Timesaver Elementary Listening

Edited by Judith Greet

Teacher's reference key

Time

A small clock on each page tells you approximately how long each activity should take.

Level

The number of stars on each page tells you the level of each activity

Students with one-two years of English

Students with two–three years of English

Listening tracks

There are two CDs. The top number relates to the CD; the lower number to the track.

SCHOLASTIC

Contents

TITLE	STRUCTURE/FUNCTION/TOPIC	LISTENING ACTIVITIES	PAGE
1 A Surprise Lunch	have got	checking information; ticking yes / no; listen and draw	14-15
2 Christmas is Coming	prepositions	ticking information; completing gaps; drawing	16-17
3 The Babysitter	feelings; times	completing sentences; drawing; drawing times	18
4 The Maths Test	illness	ticking yes / no; identifying speakers	19
5 Will's T-shirt	too	choosing the correct picture	20-21
6 Vicki's Pet	embedded questions	ordering pictures	22-23
7 Travelling by Train	travel	completing sentences; ticking yes / no; writing sentences in order	24
8 Lucky Socks	must / mustn't	ordering sentences; selecting sentences	25
9 Eating Out	I'd like / I like	identifying speakers; choosing correct sentences; identifying pictures	26-27
10 Summer Holidays	going to	choosing correct pictures; matching pictures and sentences; ticking items in a list	28-29
11 The Mystery Picture	shapes / like	drawing a picture	30
12 American Festivals	adverbs of frequency	matching	31
13 England vs America	prefer	listening for adjectives	32
14 India	comparatives and superlatives	listening for numbers; ticking true or false	33
15 What Shall We Do?	suggestions and excuses	choosing correct answers; completing sentences	34
16 A Phone Call from Jamaica	reflexive pronouns	ticking the correct picture; completing sentences	35
17 Valentine's Day	questions tags	identifying speakers; gap filling	36-37
18 Guy Fawkes	joining words	reordering pictures; joining sentences	38-39
19 Holiday Plans	first conditional	matching; identifying speakers; gap filling	40-41
20 Global Warming	unless	listening for words; ticking true or false	42
21 What's Your School Like?	discussion – school life	completing a table	43
22 Beverly Hills High School	discussion – American High School	recognising meaning of numbers; adding facts	44
23 Coral Reefs	discussion – conservation	checking facts	45
24 An Interesting Country	discussion – countries	matching sentences	46-47
25 A Typical English Person	discussion – stereotypes	completing a chart; recognising functions	48
26 Fox-hunting	discussion – fox-hunting	identifying speakers; completing a word table	49

TITLE	STRUCTURES / FUNCTIONS	LISTENING ACTIVITIES	PAGE
27 Your favourite Sport	discussion – sport	completing information	50
28 The Band	discussion – dilemmas 1	comprehension questions	51
29 The End of Term	discussion – dilemmas 2	identifying speakers; ticking yes / no; comprehension questions; gap filling	52-53
30 Oliver Twist	literature; adjectives; regular past simple	checking answers; completing sentences; pronunciation	54-55
31 A Christmas Carol	literature	ticking yes / no; completing sentences	56-57
32 Robin Hood	literature; descriptions of people; irregular past simple	multiple choice	58-59
33 The Hound of the Baskervilles	literature; asking questions	gist question; ticking yes / no; completing a table	60-61
34 Romeo and Juliet	literature; joining words	answering questions; ordering pictures	62-63
35 Othello	literature	gist questions; gap filling	64-65
36 Treasure Island	literature; rhyming words	multiple choice; pronunciation	66-67

Teacher's Notes and Answers	4-13
Recording Script	68-80

Teacher's Notes

Introduction

Elementary Listening contains 36 communicative worksheets based around listenings graded at elementary level. Each self-contained lesson includes pre-listening, while listening and post-listening tasks to ensure full exploitation and understanding of each recording. Worksheets can be selected by structure, discussion topic or literature and will act as a useful supplement to any elementary coursebook. Answers are included in the Teacher's Notes.

1 A Surprise Lunch (pages 14-15)

Listening aims: Listening for gist – checking information; **Listening for specific information** – ticking yes / no, listen and draw

New vocabulary: crisps, muffin, jealous, boring, roll, ham

Pre-listening

1 Elicit what food students can see in the pictures. Teach any new vocabulary or extend it by asking for examples of fruit and vegetables. Encourage them to create word webs for fruit and vegetables.

Monitor as the students discuss the questions. All the questions are in the past simple – check that they are using the tense correctly.

This can lead to a general discussion about eating healthily and giving advice to those who do not eat sensibly.

2 Elicit students' preferences about the lunch boxes. Ask students what they would like in a lunch box. You could also discuss if they think having a 'lunch box' meal rather than a hot meal is better.

Listening

3 Explain that Max and Robbie are discussing their lunch boxes in this listening. Students read through the statements to make sure they understand. Check answers. Play the first part of the recording twice.

Answers: a) Yes b) No c) Yes d) No e) No f) No

4 Get students to describe Max's brother. Ask what they think the relationship between the brothers is like – perhaps they argue quite a bit. Elicit ideas from the students about Max's brother's plans. They then listen to check.

Answer: He makes a spider and chocolate spread sandwich.

5 After students have drawn their pictures they can compare their answers with a partner. Each recording is repeated.

Answers: Max - an apple, a chocolate bar, a bottle of water and a cheese sandwich; **Jennie** - a banana, some crisps, some Coke, and a salad sandwich; **Robbie** - an apple, a yoghurt, a cake and a sandwich.

Post-listening

6 Go through the example with the students before they play in pairs. Monitor and take a note of any problems. Ask students who came up with the strangest sandwich.

2 Christmas is Coming (pages 16-17)

Listening aims: Listening for specific information – ticking information; completing gaps

New vocabulary: tinsel, decoration, cracker, angel, mini-disc player, wardrobe

Pre-listening

1 Students match the pictures to find the words. Check. Elicit other words connected to Christmas from the students. Encourage them to think about how to record their vocabulary. In this case they could have a page in their vocabulary books connected to Christmas. They could create sentences about themselves using the new words.

Answers: a) angel b) present c) decoration d) tinsel
e) cracker f) turkey

Listening

2 Ask students when they are given presents. Are they always a surprise? Do they try to find out what they are? Check students know all the prepositions. Play the recording through once. Students check their answers with a partner. Play the recording again to check. Check answers.

Answers: They looked in his parent's bedroom, under the bed, under the stairs, behind the sofa and in the lounge.

3 Play the recording straight through and then play with pauses after each speaker to give students time to write. Check answers.

Answers: 1) doing 2) at 3) shirt 4) for 5) your 6) shirt
7) Playstation 8) fantastic

4 Play the recording through twice if necessary. Give students time to draw the items in place. Check answers.

Answers: Students should draw: CD/Playstation <u>on</u> the wardrobe. Perfume <u>in</u> the drawers. Chocolates <u>behind</u> the wardrobe.

Post-listening

5 Check students know how to play noughts and crosses by having a game with one of them on the board. In this game they will get their nought or cross if they give a correct sentence – you are the judge. Divide the class into two teams. If you have a large group, you can divide them into small groups of four to play each other.

3 The Babysitter (page 18)

Listening aims: Listening for specific information – completing sentences, drawing, drawing times.

New vocabulary: babysit, pocket money, bedtime, frightened, bored, spider, sleepy

Pre-listening

1 Ask a few questions to find out what frightens students. Check they understand the vocabulary before doing the exercise. Then read through the examples, noting the plural and singular verbs, and give students time to write or practise their sentences. Elicit examples from the students.

Listening

2 Ask students if they ever go babysitting. Do they like doing it? Why/Why not? Have they ever had any problems when babysitting? Give them time to read through the sentences before listening. Play the recording twice. Check answers.

Answers: a) £30.00 b) money c) he wants d) mobile phone
e) orange juice; chocolate bar f) a game; reads g) 9.30
h) asleep/sleeping

3 Explain what the students have to do and play the recording. Let them compare drawings. You can then ask different students to draw them on the board to check the answers.

Answers: Students should draw: 1 angry face; 2 sleepy face; 3 happy face; 4 hungry face.

4 Play the recording, leaving a pause for students to draw the times. Again ask students to draw the times on the board to check the answers.

Answers: 1 seven o'clock; 2 ten past seven; 3 quarter past seven; 4 twenty past seven; 5 twenty past eight; 6 half past eight.

Post-listening

5 Students can discuss in small groups and then report back to the class.

4 The Maths Test (page 19)

Listening aims: Listening for specific information – ticking Yes / No; Listening for gist – identifying speakers

New vocabulary: test, stomach ache, appendicitis, medicine, feel sick

Pre-listening

1 Let students work in pairs to do this exercise. Check answers.
Answers: 1 a 2 a 3 a 4 b 5 a 6 a

Listening

2 Students read through the sentences before listening. Play the recording once. Check answers.
Answers: a) No b) No c) Yes d) No e) No f) No g) Yes h) Yes i) Yes

3 Play the recording again, giving students time to read the sentences first. Check answers. Elicit from students why the characters say these lines.
Answers: a) M b) D c) W d) D e) M f) W

Post-listening

4 Read through the excuses with the class. Let them work in pairs to think of another excuse. Then they can swap sheets with another pair to answer the questions. Elicit some of the new excuses – the class can vote on their favourite.

In pairs, students practise the situation. Choose a few to act their situation in front of the class.

5 Will's T-shirt (pages 20-21)

Listening aims: Listening for specific information – choosing the correct picture

New vocabulary: horrible, changing room, charity shop, accessories, earrings, bracelet, belt, wrist band, sunglasses, rings, necklace

Pre-listening

1 Give students about four minutes to discuss in pairs or small groups what they would wear. Teach any new vocabulary.

Listening

2 Give students time to read the questions and look at the pictures. Play the recording twice. Check answers.
Answers: 1 C 2 A 3 B 4 C 5 A 6 B

Post-listening

3 Students work in pairs to find seven problems. Elicit answers.
Answers: a) The hat is too big. b) The jacket is too small.
c) The chocolate is too expensive. d) The car is too old.
e) The balloon is too high. f) The cat is too fat.
g) The man is too tall.

6 Vicki's Pet (pages 22-23)

Listening aims: Listening for gist – ordering pictures

New vocabulary: hamster, tortoise, guinea pig, stick insect, seed

Pre-listening

1 Let students try to fill as much of the puzzle as possible. They can then use dictionaries to help them. Check answers. Discuss the mystery pet. Ask students if they have any strange pets.
Answers: 1 tortoise 2 hamster 3 parrot 4 rabbit
5 stick insect 6 kitten 7 puppy 8 goldfish 9 guinea pig
The mystery pet is a tarantula.

Listening

2 Give the students time to look at the pictures before listening to the recording.
Answers: 1 c 2 f 3 a 4 e 5 b 6 d

Post-listening

3 These embedded questions might be quite difficult for the students. You need to take them through the changes step by step. Get them to ask you a question, saying *I want to go to the bank but I don't know where it is. What shall I ask?* Elicit *Where is the bank, please?* Write it on the board and discuss how questions are formed. Ask them to try to add *Do you know* to the beginning of the sentence. Write the correct form on the board and point out the changes, i.e. *Do you know where the bank is?* Then get them to add *I don't know* to the beginning of the question in the same way i.e. *I don't know where the bank is.* Practise with the examples in the exercise. These are only with the verb *to be* or modals. You could extend this to using *do / does / did*.
Answers: a) I don't know how you can drink only water.
b) I don't know how you can eat that disgusting food. c) I don't know what time it is. d) I don't know where Charlie is. e) I don't know how much the new Linkin Park CD is. f) I don't know where Vicki was yesterday. g) I don't know why Will isn't here.
h) I don't know what Vicki's favourite film is.

7 Travelling by train (page 24)

Listening aims: Listening for specific information – completing sentences, ticking Yes / No, writing sentences in order

New vocabulary: conductor, ticket, pilot, seatbelt, driver, to take off, to get on/off, to land, platform, skateboarding, embarrassing

Pre-listening

1 Explain how a venn diagram works if necessary. Give the students time to complete it in pairs. They can use dictionaries if possible, preferably English-English ones. Check answers.
Answers: Train – conductor, ticket office, driver, tracks, guard, platform; **Both** – single ticket, return ticket, seat, engine, to get on, to get off; **Plane** – pilot, seatbelt, to take off, runway, steward, to land

Listening

2 Ask students if they like travelling by train. Why / Why not? Play the first part of the recording twice. Check answers.
Answers: a) skateboarding b) visits his aunt and uncle
c) flowers d) far; boring e) embarrassed f) a single g) £3.60

3 Give the students time to read the sentences before listening to the recording. Play the recording twice.
Answers: a) Yes b) No c) No d) Yes e) No

4 Elicit a dialogue from the students about buying a plane ticket. Give students time to read through the sentences and reorder before listening to check.
Answers: see Recording script

Post-listening

5 This can be set as homework. Discuss the questions with the class. Write any new vocabulary up on the board.

8 Lucky Socks (page 25)

Listening aims: Listening for specific information: ordering sentences; selecting sentences

New vocabulary: detention, cheeky, champions, chewing gum

Pre-listening

1 Let students discuss the different pictures and elicit if they have a lucky charm which they take into exams with them.

Listening

2 Give students time to read through the sentences before listening to the recording and reordering the sentences.
Answers: j, c, k, g, b, a, e, i, l, d, f, h

3 Give students time to read through the rules first. After they have listened, ask them if they think the rules are good.

Post-listening

4 Students write their own rules in groups. Perhaps you could also write your rules and then compare them with the students' ones and create a set of class rules which have been agreed on by everyone.

9 Eating Out (pages 26-27)

Listening aims: Listening for gist – identifying speakers; Listening for specific information – choosing correct sentences; identifying pictures

New vocabulary: vanilla, peach, mint, toffee, pistachio, starter, dessert

Pre-listening

1 Students work in pairs to solve the anagrams. They can make up more of their own to give to other pairs if you wish.
Answers: a) mint b) toffee c) banana d) raspberry e) peach f) vanilla g) strawberry h) chocolate

Listening

2 Check students know all the vocabulary on the menu before they listen.
Answers: Victoria: Green salad, Fish, Strawberry ice cream.
David: Melon, Four cheese pizza, Chocolate ice cream.

3 Students can practise saying the sentences before they listen to them. Check the answers.
Answers: 1a 2b 3b 4a

Post-listening

4 Give students about five minutes to create their menus. Students role play being the waiter and customers.

Listening

5 Check students know all the vocabulary before they listen.

10 Summer Holidays (pages 28-29)

Listening aims: Listening for gist – choosing correct pictures; Listening for specific information – matching pictures and sentences; ticking items in a list

New vocabulary: rollercoaster, dodgems, dart, target, cuddly toy, oil, flip-flops

Pre-listening

1 Teach any new vocabulary. Students discuss the different rides and choose their favourites. Elicit preferences from the class with reasons. Ask them to describe the scariest rides they have been on.

Listening

2 Discuss the pictures with the class before they listen to the recording and teach any relevant vocabulary. Play the recording twice if necessary.
Answers: 1b 2b 3b 4b 5b 6a

3 Elicit what each picture is showing before students listen and then play the recording once only. Check answers.
Answers: Monday = c Tuesday = e Wednesday = d Thursday = g Friday = b Saturday = a Sunday = f

4 Ask students to match the words and pictures before they listen. Play the recording twice. Check answers.
Answers: Students should tick: sunglasses, sun oil, CD player, flip flops

Post-listening

5 Students make their own lists and then compare with a partner. They have to look at both lists together and choose only seven to take. They have to try to persuade each other that their chioce is best.

11 The Mystery Picture (page 30)

Listening aims: Listening for specific information – drawing a picture

New vocabulary: round, handle, triangle, star, rectangle, spiral, hexagon, diamond, oval

Pre-listening

1 Give students five minutes to find as many examples of each shape as possible.
Answer: circle = 16 half circle = 12 diamond = 2 oval = 5 hexagon = 7 triangle = 4 square = 4 rectangle = 15 spiral = 2 star = 6

Listening

2 Play the recording through once and then play it again, pausing after every sentence for students to draw the picture. Give them a few minutes at the end to complete it. Let them compare their pictures, then play the recording again so they can decide whether to change anything or not. Ask different students to come to the board and draw the correct picture.
Answer:

Post-listening

3 Using the picture that they drew in exercise 2, elicit sentences from the students eg The moon looks like a letter 'C'. Students work in pairs to say what the pictures here look like – they should create as many answers as they can. There is no correct answer.

4 This is a short exercise to practise the different ways we use *like*. Make sure that students do not include the word *like* in answers b) and c) (e.g. b) It's warm. c) He's tall and strict.)

12 American Festivals (page 31)

Listening aims: Listening for gist – matching

New vocabulary: festival, monster, nasty surprise, bad habits, religious, proud

Pre-listening

1 Students discuss the questions in small groups or pairs before reporting back to the class. Write up any new vocabulary on the board.

Listening

2 Discuss the different days with the students, eliciting some information about each one. They can use the pictures to help them. Give them vocabulary. They then listen to do the exercise. Play the recording once. Check their answers.
Answers: 1 Halloween 2 New Year's Day 3 Thanksgiving
4 Independence Day

3 Give the students a minute to read through the questions before playing the recording again.
Answers: a) H b) N c) T d) H e) N f) T g) H h) T i) ID
j) H k) T l) ID m) ID

Post-listening

4 Students have to decide on the correct word order to solve this puzzle. When they have got the answer, elicit the rule about word order with adverbs of frequency (they come before the verb *to be*, *to have* and modals; they come after other verbs).
Answers: a) is always b) usually have c) sometimes go
d) are often e) always speaks   The celebration is Labor Day.

13 England vs America (page 32)

Listening aims: Listening for specific information – listening for adjectives

New vocabulary: amazing, guns, dangerous, lucky, exciting

Pre-listening

1 Give students three to four minutes to think of adjectives to describe the US and Britain. Ask if they have visited either country. Would they like to move to the US or Britain?

Listening

2 Play the recording through twice and elicit answers. After they have done the exercise, ask them which adjectives they would use to describe their countries. Elicit other adjectives to describe them.
Answers: England is too small, safe, boring; America is too big, amazing, dangerous, exciting

Post-listening

3 Go through the example with the class. They practise in pairs. Encourage them to add an explanation like the example.

4 Young people tend to use 'cool' to describe things that are good. Although your students can use the word in speech, they should know other adjectives so as to make their writing more interesting.
Possible answers: fantastic / wonderful; beautiful / gorgeous; friendly; interesting / trendy; delicious / tasty; exciting

14 India (page 33)

Listening aims: Listening for specific information – numbers; ticking true or false

New vocabulary: religion, curry, exercise, regions, panthers, cheetah, laws, film-making

Pre-listening

1 Students can work in pairs to complete the exercise. Check answers and elicit other facts from the students about India.
Answers: 1f 2a 3g 4b (formerly Bombay) 5c 6d 7e

Listening

2 Read through the numbers and let students guess what they might refer to. Play the recording through once.
Answers: a) number of people living in Mumbai
b) population c) number of languages d) number of tigers

3 Students read through the sentences before listening again.
Answers: a) F b) F c) F d) T e) F f) F g) T

Post-listening

4 Monitor as the students are working ensuring that they are using the correct form of the comparative adjective.

15 What Shall We Do? (page 34)

Listening aims: Listening for gist – choosing the correct answers; Listening for specific information – completing sentences

New vocabulary: ballet, rugby, yoga, in-line hockey, go-karting

Pre-listening

1 Students sit in groups of eight and each asks a question eg *Do you hang out with your friends after school?* They indicate the answers on the questionnaire. Elicit sentences from each group about the different questions, e.g. *Six of us hang out with friends after school; two of us don't hang out with friends after school.*

Listening

2 Give students two minutes to read through the table. Play the recording through once. Check answers.
Answers: 2a 3a 4a 5b; Jennifer wants to watch TV.

3 Play the recording again. Students work in pairs to complete the sentences.
Answers: a) Why don't you come b) Let's go c) How about going d) Shall we go e) Do you want to go

Post-listening

4 Elicit ways of suggesting from exercise 3. Elicit any other ways of suggesting eg *What about going ...?* Students take turns to make suggestions and give excuses. Monitor as they work. Correct any mistakes at the end. Choose a few groups to perform their dialogue in front of the class. You could vote on the best excuses.

16 A Phone Call from Jamaica (page 35)

Listening aims: Listening for gist – ticking the correct picture; Listening for specific information – completing sentences

New vocabulary: burn, sunbathe, honeymoon, package holiday, activity holiday

Pre-listening

1 Give students about three minutes to solve the anagrams. There is no picture for the package holiday. Explain any new vocabulary.
Answers: a) cruise b) camping c) skiing d) package
e) sailing f) activity g) walking h) honeymoon

Listening

2 Check any new vocabulary by getting the students to describe what they can see in the pictures. Play the recording once. Check answers.
Answers: 1 B 2 B 3 A

3 Pause the recording regularly so that students have time to complete the sentences.
Answers: See Recording script.

Post-listening
4 Let the students work in pairs. Check the answers.
Answers: Students should remove the reflexive pronoun from the following sentences: a, b, d, e, i, j

17 Valentine's Day (pages 36-37)

Listening aims: Listening for specific information – matching questions, gap filling
New vocabulary: waste money

Pre-listening
1 Discuss with students what they think of Valentine's Day. Let them look at the pictures in small groups and report back to the class. Elicit other suggestions for presents.

Listening
2 Give students a minute to read through the questions before answering them. Check answers.
Answers: a) Kate   b) Simon   c) Simon   d) Simon   e) Kate
f) Simon   g) Simon   h) Kate

3 Students can complete the dialogue with the question tags first and then listen to check.
Answers: 1 doesn't it?   2 isn't it?   3 did you?   4 do you?
5 didn't you?   6 are you?

4 This is pronunciation practice before they do the next exercise. Check that they are getting the intonation correct.

Post-listening
5 Go through the example with the class. Students have to complete the table before working with a partner. Monitor and listen to the intonation.

18 Guy Fawkes (pages 38-39)

Listening aims: Listening for gist – reordering pictures; Listening for specific information – joining sentences
New vocabulary: fireworks, Catholic, cellar, gunpowder, warn, relative, torture, arrest, confess

Pre-listening
1 Discuss with the class when they go to see fireworks. Do they like them? Do they think they are a good way to help celebrate an occasion?

Listening
2 Discuss the pictures before the students listen, teaching any new vocabulary. Play the recording twice if necessary.
Answers: The correct order is: 2, 5, 3, 1, 4

3 Students listen again to find out how they can join the sentences. Let them discuss their answers in pairs before checking as a class.
Answers: 1 Guy Fawkes was a Catholic and he hated the King;
2 Guy Fawkes joined a group of men who wanted to kill the king; 3 One of the men had a relative who often visited the Houses of Parliament; 4 He warned his relative about the plan and his relative warned King James; 5 When Guy Fawkes entered the cellar on the night of November 5th, the King's men were already there; 6 They wanted to know the names of the other men so they tortured Guy Fawkes until he confessed.

Post-listening
4 This is a similar exercise to the previous one.
Answers: a) who   b) so   c) and   d) When   e) When   f) who
g) and   h) so

5 Students can work in pairs to match the questions and answers.
Answers: 1g   2d   3a   4i   5e   6h   7f   8c   9b
The man who stopped the conspiracy was Lord Monteagle. He warned the King.

19 Holiday Plans (pages 40-41)

Listening aims: Listening for gist – matching; Listening for specific information – identifying speakers; gap filling
New vocabulary: curry, spicy, soldiers, art gallery, canal, surfing, passport, embassy

Pre-listening
1 Let students discuss in pairs and then check answers. Let students make some of their own puzzles up.
Answers: b) Thailand   c) China   d) South Africa   e) Italy
f) Greece

Listening
2 Students have to listen and write down who mentions which place as a possible holiday destination. Play the recording once.
Answers: Paul – India, Australia, England;
Sally Ann – America, Scotland, Ireland

3 Play the recording again and then check answers. Students write the remaining three conditional sentences.
Answers: a) S   b) P   c) P   d) S
b) If his brother doesn't invite him, Paul will go to India.
c) If he can't take a month off work, Paul won't go to India.
d) If the weather is nice, Sally Ann will go to Scotland or Ireland.

Post-listening
4 Let students work in pairs to think of possible answers. Accept all correct answers.
Possible answers: b) If I am ill, I will use my insurance and go to see a doctor; c) If someone steals my money, I will report it to the police and borrow some from my cousin; d) If we can't find a hotel to stay in, we'll sleep in the car; e) If our car breaks down, we'll take it to a garage; f) If I miss my plane home, I'll get the next one.

5 Play the song through for the students and ask them if they like it – why/why not? Give out the sheet and ask them to try and complete the gaps. Play it through again so they can check their answers and complete any remaining gaps.
Answers: 1) ends   2) relax   3) spend   4) catch   5) come
6) travel   7) sit   8) having   9) are

20 Global Warming (page 42)

Listening aims: Listening for specific information – listening for words; Listening for gist – ticking true or false
New vocabulary: recycle, compost heap, eco-issues, litter, neighbourhood, global warming, temperature, environment, flood, melt, ice cap, pollution, carbon dioxide, rainforest, cut down

Pre-listening
1 You may like to teach some of the new vocabulary first. Go through the questionnaire with the students to make sure they understand it and introduce the new vocabulary at the same time. They can then answer the questions and check their scores. Elicit who is the greenest in the class. Establish their reaction to this and whether they think it is important and why / why not.

Listening
2 Play the recording through once while the students tick the words they hear. Check the answers.
Answers: Students should have ticked: temperatures, degrees, sea levels, flooded, air, pollution (not rainforest because the speaker says rainforests)

3 Students can try to answer the questions before they listen again if you wish. Let them do it in pairs then listen to check their answers.
Answers: a) F b) F c) T d) T e) F

Post-listening
4 Remind students that *unless* means *if not*. They need to study the positive and negative parts of the sentences before transforming them. Check answers.
Answers: a) Unless we save fuel, there won't be enough for the future; b) Unless we protect our lakes and river, they will become polluted; c) Unless we stop cutting down rainforests, the hole in the ozone layer will get bigger; d) Unless we stop global warming, temperatures will rise further.

5 Students work in groups before sharing ideas with the whole class.

21 What's Your School Like? (page 43)
Listening aims: Listening for gist – completing a table
New vocabulary: best, worst

Pre-listening
1 Give the students time working individually to complete the diagram.
Answers:

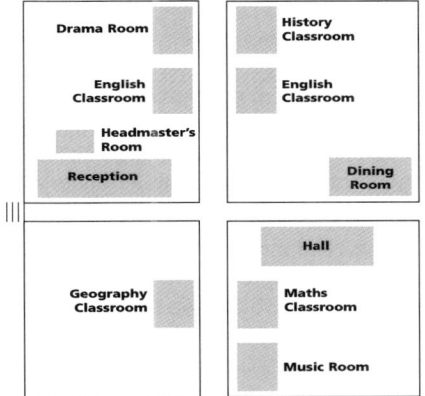

(Diagram showing: Drama Room, History Classroom, English Classroom, English Classroom, Headmaster's Room, Reception, Dining Room, Hall, Geography Classroom, Maths Classroom, Music Room)

Listening
2 Students read through the chart before listening twice to the recording.
Answer:

	Kate	Simon	Adam	Jennifer
Do you like going to school?	yes	yes	no	yes
What do you like best about school?	school trips	drama lessons	sport	music club
What's the worst thing about school?	homework	maths lessons	exams	school food
What are your teachers like?	nice	too strict	OK	friendly

Post-listening
3 This exercise looks at word order. Add some more examples of your own which your students often make mistakes with.
Answers: b) I don't like science at all; c) The subject I like best is biology; d) I always enjoy sport; e) I don't like any of my other lessons; f) Most of my lessons are interesting.

4 Students complete the sentences and compare their answers with a partner before sharing their ideas with the class.

5 Have a discussion about home education. Ask the students if they know of anyone who is educated at home. Ask why they think some parents choose to do this. In groups, they think of the pros and cons then decide which one they would choose. They then discuss with the rest of the class.

22 Beverly Hills High School (page 44)
Listening aims: Listening for specific information – recognising meaning of numbers; adding facts
New vocabulary: grade, semester, drama, college, glamorous, radio station

Pre-listening
1 The vocabulary in this exercise is a little difficult. However, the first letter is given in each case so students will be able to work out the words. Give them about five minutes for this exercise working in pairs. They will then work out the sentence about the students – ask them why they think they become so famous.
Answers: a) grade b) semester c) prom d) yearbook e) freshman f) sophomore
Kids often become very famous.

Listening
2 Read through the numbers with the students first. Play the recording once. Check answers and discuss the listening.

3 Choose students to read the sentences, eliciting views from the other students. Students listen again and find three more facts.
Possible answers: It's about 25 kilometres from Los Angeles. Some of the students have famous parents. It's also good for sports. You don't have to be American to go to the school.

Post-listening
4 Ask students to work in groups. Discuss what their school is like and note the differences. They then decide which school they would prefer to go to and why.

23 Coral Reefs (page 45)
Listening aims: Listen for specific information – checking facts
New vocabulary: coral reefs, damaged, extinct, disappear, disturb, protect, salty, coast, medicine, hurricanes

Pre-listening
1 Students work in pairs to complete the puzzle.
Answers: a)T b)F c)T d)T e)F f)F g)T h)T i)T (Australia)

Listening
2 Students read through the statements – check vocabulary.
Answers: Students should tick a, c and e

Post-listening
3 This exercise practises the present continuous to show things that are happening continuously. Students might be able to come up with other sentences related to the environment.
Answers: b) are getting c) are cutting down d) are damaging e) are thinking f) is becoming

4 Students discuss the sentences and give their opinions.

24 An Interesting Country (pages 46-47)
Listening aims: Listening for gist – matching sentences
New vocabulary: poet, instrument, invent, lake, turnip, checked, chopped

Pre-listening
1 Elicit suggestions about the pictures – they are all related to Scotland. Ask students if they know anything else about Scotland.

Listening
2 Give students a minute to look at the sentences before they listen. Play the recording twice. Students can compare their answers before checking as a class. Look at the completed sentences with the students and elicit what word can be used instead of *that* (*which*). Ask if *that* can be used instead of *who* (yes, it can because these are defining clauses).
Answers: 1g 2d 3b 4c 5h 6a 7e 8f

Post-listening
3 Go through the example with the class and elicit other things Italy is famous for eg Leaning tower of Pisa, art galleries, wine, etc. Let them work in pairs to say what each country is famous for. The countries are: France, Britain, Egypt, USA, Australia.

Listening
4 Explain some vocabulary before they listen. Some of the more difficult vocabulary includes: liver, heart, animal fat, turnip. Students listen once. Check answers.
Answers: 1e 2c 3b 4a 5d

Post-listening
5 Give students two or three minutes to complete the table, working in pairs. Then give them another three minutes to add other foods to the lists. Check answers.
Answers: Countable – vegetable
Both – turnip, potato, chicken, haggis (in all cases, when you go to the shop you can buy 1 or more than one and you can count the number you have bought – *I went to the shop and bought a turnip, four potatoes, two chickens and a haggis*; when the food is cooked and on the plate, it is no longer countable – *I ate some turnip, some potato, some haggis and some chicken*. In this case, the nouns are not in the plural).
Uncountable – meat, animal fat, beef

6 Students can work in groups to prepare ideas for their posters. You could give the preparation of this task or the actual task for homework.

25 A Typical English Person (page 48)

Listening aims: Listening for gist – completing a chart;
Listening for specific information – recognising functions
New vocabulary: typical, neither

Pre-listening
1 Encourage students to write as much as they can under each heading. Give them a time limit, e.g. three minutes.

Listening
2 Play the recording through once. Ask them who they think is more typical of English people – Tom or Helen.
Answers: Tom – coffee, fish and chips, football, cat, the weather; **Helen** – coffee, curry, tennis, cat, the weather

3 Give students time to read through the functions and try to write some of the expressions. Let them work in pairs. Then play the recording again. Check answers.
Answers: a) What do you think Tom? b) So do I. c) Really?
d) What about football?; Well, what about animals?
e) don't you? f) Neither do I.

Post-listening
4 Students discuss in pairs before discussing as a class.

26 Fox-hunting (page 49)

Listening aims: Listening for specific information – identifying speakers; completing a word table
New vocabulary: trap, cruel, chase, escape, painful, poison, pollute, natural

Pre-listening
1 Students work in small groups to give their opinions. Group leaders give the group's views. Discuss as a class.

Listening
2 Students read through the statements. Play the recording twice.
Answers: a) W b) S c) W d) W e) S f) S

3 Students try to listen for the missing words on the recording. Play it through once more.
Answers: cruel beautiful painful poison dangerous disease

Post-listening
4 Students read through the statements and then discuss their views in small groups. Monitor as they are discussing. Discuss any problems when they have finished. Open the discussion out to the class.

27 Your Favourite Sport (page 50)

Listening aims: Listening for specific information – completing information
New vocabulary: racquet, goggles, karate, shoulder pads, helmets, goal post, championship, pitch

Pre-listening
1 In this exercise, students have to recognise the sports and then match with the correct verb. Let pupils work in pairs. Discuss the equipment needed for the sports and teach any new vocabulary. Let students add any other sports to the lists.
Answers: play – badminton, squash, basketball, football, golf, tennis; **do** – karate, gymnastics; **go** – fishing, swimming, riding

Listening
2 Let students read through the information before listening. Play the recording through twice.
Answers: a) five b) two, twelve c) 15 d) 49 e) 100
f) seven g) four h) 2,500
Favourite sports: Kate – basketball; Simon – American football; Jennifer – tennis; Adam - football

Post-listening
3 Suggest that students think of a sport that they know well and try to change some of the rules and give the sport a new name.

4 Read through the information with the students, explaining any new vocabulary. Ask them if they know what any other sportsmen earn – add it to their table. Ask the class to say if the sportsmen deserve what they earn or not. Let each group discuss their views with each other. Then let them work in smaller groups, with some students supporting the salaries and some against. Let them have a discussion – does anyone change their mind? Ask groups to tell the class what happened in their discussion.

28 The Band (page 51)

Listening aims: Listening for specific information
–comprehension questions
New vocabulary: charity, raise money, concert, poster, loads of money

Pre-listening

1 Discuss what charities the students have heard of; they then answer the questions in groups. Discuss their answers.

Listening

2 Students read through the questions before listening. Play Part 1 twice.
Answers: a) animal charities; b) They're going to have a concert for the charity.; c) Dave; d) Natasha; e) do posters to advertise the concert; f) Angels; g) Natasha can't sing.

Post-listening

3 Students discuss the dilemma in groups. Ask for a vote on which option they choose. Students will find out what they did in Part 2.

Listening

4 Students read through the next set of questions. Play Part 2 twice.
Answers: a) They persuaded her to do something else; b) Yes; c) The best band in the area; d) Yes; e) A musician from Gameboy. He wants Dave to join them.

5 Students discuss the dilemma in groups. Then listen to find out what Dave did. Do students think he chose the correct option?

29 The End of Term (pages 52-53)

Listening aims: Listening for specific information – identifying speakers; ticking yes / no; comprehension questions; gap filling

New vocabulary: sprinting, high jump, practice, fed up, cheer, popcorn

Pre-listening

1 Students do the questionnaire and discuss their answers with a partner.

Listening

2 Students read through the sentences and then listen to Part 1. Play it through twice. Elicit why Jane says each of these things.
Answers: Jane says – b, d, g, h

Post-listening

3 Students discuss the dilemma in small groups and give their opinions to the class. They will find out what she actually does in the next part.

Listening

4 Students read through the sentences and then listen to Part 2.
Answers: a) Yes b) No c) No d) No e) No f) No g) No h) Yes

Post-listening

5 Students discuss the dilemma in small groups and give their opinions to the class. They will find out what she actually does in the next part.

Listening

6 Students read through the sentences and then listen to Part 3.
Answers: a) She tells Andy she can't go out with him.
b) and c) Student's own answers   d) Yes   e) Yes

7 Play the song through for the students just to listen to. Do they like it? Play it though again while students complete the gaps.
Answers: 1 swimming   2 eat   3 drink   4 singing   5 have
6 relax   7 walking   8 watch   9 get   10 leave   11 go   12 play

30 Oliver Twist (pages 54-55)

Background information: Charles Dickens lived from 1812 to 1870. He wrote about social problems and poor conditions of working people in Victorian times. He wrote 15 major novels. He himself came from a poor family and was sent to work in a factory when he was nine years old. He suffered badly in the terrible conditions and used his own experiences in his writing. He started writing Oliver Twist in 1837. Many films have been made of the novel.

Listening aims: Listening for gist – checking answers;
Listening for specific information – completing sentences; pronunciation

New vocabulary: locket, punishment, kidnap, gold, wallet, library

Pre-listening

1 Ask if any of the students know the story of Oliver Twist – perhaps they have seen a film. Elicit what they know and write any new words on the board. Discuss the background information with them. Students can work in pairs to complete the puzzle.
Answers: 1 wallet 2 stole 3 picture 4 bank 5 neck 6 thief

2 Students could use dictionaries to help them write definitions of the words. Give them some examples of words they can use as the mystery word. It could be a word related to what they have learnt about the story so far, e.g. steal; or it could be something completely different, e.g. monkey.

Listening

3 Working in small groups, students think of two adjectives for each character. Alternatively divide the class into four and assign each group one character for whom they have to think of adjectives. Elicit adjectives from the class and accept all sensible answers. Write them on the board under each name. Do not say if they are right or wrong.
Possible answers: Oliver – sad, thin, young, poor; The Artful Dodger – cheeky, clever, naughty; Fagin – ugly, evil, scruffy, mean, greedy; Mr Brownlow – smart, well-dressed, rich, kind

Play the recording and ask the students to listen and decide if they have got the correct adjectives. Do they want to change any? Can they add any more? Explain any new vocabulary at this point, e.g. workhouse.

4 Students read through the text to complete the gaps with the verbs before they listen again and check the answers.
Answers: 1 lived   2 asked   3 decided   4 walked   5 stayed
6 wanted   7 looked after   8 visited   9 pushed   10 showed
11 tried   12 promised

5 Practise the examples with the class first. Point out the fact that when verbs end in unvoiced consonants i.e. sh, s, f, p, k, x, ch, the 'ed' ending will be pronounced as 't'; when the verb ends in 't' or 'd', the 'ed' ending is 'id'; all the others take the 'd' sound.
Students listen and write the verbs they hear in the correct columns.
Answers: 'd': tried, lived, showed, stayed; 't': walked, promised, pushed, asked, looked after; 'id': visited, wanted, decided

Post-listening

6 Give students three minutes to match the sentence halves. Check answers.
Answers: 1d   2a   3e   4b   5c

Then ask students to substitute the word 'that' with another relative pronoun, i.e. who or which.

Answers: a) who   b) which   c) which   d) who   e) which

Students can then write other sentences about the story using *who* or *which*, e.g. Mr Brownlow was a kind man who looked after Oliver.; Oliver climbed through a window which was very small.

7 Give students time to write their reactions to the stories. Students can do this in groups if they wish.

31 A Christmas Carol (pages 56-57)

Background information: See Activity 30 for information on Charles Dickens. In the 1840s, Dickens wrote a series of Christmas Books, the most famous of which is *A Christmas Carol*. He decided to write a Chrsitmas story to highlight the plight of the poor and to appeal for better-off people to help. There was severe economic depression in England in the 1840s.

Listening aims: Listening for specific information – ticking yes / no sentences; completing sentences

New vocabulary: mean, ghost, fiancée, graveyard

Pre-listening

1 Discuss why people have holidays on certain days and what they do. Elicit other holidays. Discuss the benefits of holidays – people relax, they visit their families, they enjoy themselves.

Listening

2 Discuss the pictures with the class and elicit from students what part each character might play in the story. If they do not know the story ask them which character they think the ghost might haunt.
Students read through the sentences before they listen. Give them a minute to do this. Play the tape twice.

Answers: a) No   b) No   c) Yes   d) No   e) No   f) Yes   g) No   h) Yes   i) No   j) Yes

3 Explain that the sentences are about the first two ghosts. Students work in pairs to complete the sentences.

Answers: 1 party   2 dancing   3 sad   4 ghost   5 house   6 food   7 happy   8 ill

Post-listening

4 Give students time to give their opinion of the story.

32 Robin Hood (pages 58-59)

Background information: Robin Hood is supposed to have been born in the 12th century. The story is that Robin Hood was an outlaw who poached the King's deer in Sherwood Forest and stole money from rich people to give to the poor. He not only constantly tricked the Sheriff of Nottingham but he also highlighted the corrupt nature of some churchmen and officials.

Listening aims: Listening for specific information – multiple choice

New vocabulary: deer, prison, prisoner, ropes, forest, bridge, castle

Pre-listening

1 Elicit any information students know about Robin Hood. Let them complete the exercise before checking the answers.
Answers: Robin Hood – d, h   The Sheriff of Nottingham – c, e   John Little – a, g   Friar Tuck – b, f

Listening

2 Give students one or two minutes to read through the questions before listening. Play the recording twice.
Answers: 1A   2B   3B   4B   5A   6A   7B   8A

3 Students listen again to find out what they can about Maid Marian.
Answers: She was beautiful. Her father was a knight. She married Robin Hood.

Post-listening

4 Let students work individually at first. They can then check their answers with a partner before checking as a class.
Answers: a) died   b) grew up   c) put   d) won   e) became   f) stole   g) gave   h) got   i) caught   j) fought

5 Let students discuss this in groups and then each group can tell their legend to the rest of the class.

33 The Hound of the Baskervilles (pages 60-61)

Background: Sir Arthur Conan Doyle (1859 - 1930) was famous as the author of *Sherlock Holmes*. However, he had various other jobs during his life. He worked on board an Arctic whaler as a doctor, was a war correspondent in Egypt, and even stood, unsuccessfully, for Parliament. He trained as a medical doctor and got his degree from Edinburgh University in 1881.

Sherlock Holmes' most famous case, *The Hound of the Baskervilles*, was set on foggy Dartmoor. The first episodes of *The Hound of the Baskervilles* were published in 1901. This book is said to be Conan Doyle's best novel. Sherlock Holmes' assistant was Doctor Watson to whom he always said, 'Elementary, my dear Watson.'

Listening aims: Listening for gist – gist question;
Listening for specific information – ticking yes / no questions; completing a table

New vocabulary: hound, devil, footprint, moor, swamp, strange, detective

Pre-listening

1 Ask students if they have read any Sherlock Holmes' stories or seen any films. Do they like the stories? Why?
Let students do the exercise in pairs.
Answers: 1 d   2 e   3 f   4 c   5 a   6 b

Listening

2 Explain who the different characters in the story are. Students listen to find the answer.
Answer: 3

3 Give students time to read through the questions before they listen again. They answer the questions individually and then check with their partner. Elicit answers.
Answers: a) Yes   b) Yes   c) Yes   d) No   e) No   f) No   g) No   h) Yes   i) Yes   j) Yes   k) No   l) Yes   m) No   n) Yes

4 Let students read through the passage and try to correct the mistakes. Give them about three minutes to do it and ask how many changes they have made (there are 14 in total). Play the section for them again to check. Check answers.
Answers: A few = Many   kind = cruel   Charles = Hugo   lady = girl   loved = hated   morning = night   cellar = room   climbed = jumped   horses = hounds   police = devil   her = him   the police = people   afternoon = day   leg = neck

5 This exercise practises making questions. Students can work in pairs to write the questions and then practise asking and answering with another pair.
Answers: b) What was Hugo Baskerville like? He was cruel.
c) Who did he love? He loved a girl who hated him.   d) Where did Hugo lock the girl? He locked her in a room in Baskerville Hall.   e) What did she do? She escaped.   f) Who chased her? Hugo chased her.   g) Who did Hugo ask for help? He asked

the devil for help.   h) What chased Hugo? The devil's hounds chased him.   i) When did they find Hugo? The next day.
j) What happened to him? He was dead.

7 Play the recording twice.
Answers: Sherlock Holmes is brilliant and careful; Stapleton is horrible and clever; The hound is enormous and evil.

Post-listening
6 Discuss Sherlock Holmes with the class. Let them work in small groups to write their information.

34 Romeo and Juliet (pages 62-63)

Background information: William Shakespeare (1564 - 1616) was born in Stratford-upon-Avon. From the age of seven to about 14, he attended Stratford Grammar School receiving an excellent well-rounded education. At the age of 18 he married Anne Hathaway. He eventually left her and fled to London to become an actor. He was an excellent actor but it is as a playwright that he is remembered. He wrote 37 plays of different genres – historical romances, comedies, tragedies.

Romeo and Juliet is a romantic tragedy about a boy and a girl who fall in love. However their families hate each other bitterly. Everything goes wrong for them and they kill themselves rather than be parted. The play is set in Italy. The play starts on a Sunday morning in the middle of July; less than five days later - just before dawn on the following Thursday - it is all over.

Listening aims: Listening for gist – answering questions; picture ordering

New vocabulary: get married, in secret, poison

Pre-listening
1 Discuss with the class what they know about the play *Romeo and Juliet*. Give some background information (but do not say where it takes place – see Exercise 4), using the pictures in exercise 2.
Students work in pairs to complete the exercise.
Answers: Love – adore, to be fond of, to be crazy about, to be keen on; **Hate** – detest, can't stand, loathe, can't bear

Listening
2 With the background information you have given the students, they may be able to guess the answers to the questions before they listen. If so, write their answers on the board and then ask them to listen to check.
Answers: a) No   b) No   c) Yes   d) No

3 Students decide on the order of the pictures before listening again. Do not correct the answers until they have listened.
Answers: 1 e   2 a   3 d   4 b   5 f   6 c

Post-listening
4 Students can work in pairs to complete the exercise.
Answers: 1 because   2 because   3 so   4 because   5 so
The country is Italy.

5 Elicit details about each picture in Exercise 3 from the students so that they can retell the story. Write any useful vocabulary on the board. The story can be started in class and finished for homework.

35 Othello (pages 64-65)

Background information: See Activity 34 Teacher's Notes for information on Shakespeare.

Othello, one of Shakespeare's four great tragedies, was first performed in 1604. The character of Iago is particularly evil and his jealousy and hatred of Othello causes the tragedy.

Listening aims: Listening for gist – gist questions; **Listening for specific information** – gap filling

New vocabulary: revenge, relax, drunk, in secret, handkerchief, honest, liar

Pre-listening
1 Discuss the characters and their parts with the class. Elicit who could be jealous of who. Then look at the three pictures (wine, handkerchief and dagger) and ask if they can guess what might happen in the story.

Listening
2 Let students listen without reading the play first to see if they can establish what significance each item has.
3 Students listen again while reading the play and completing it.
Answers: 1 chose   2 hates   3 too   4 about   5 have to
6 like   7 must   8 so   9 sorry   10 agrees   11 visiting   12 not
13 about   14 met   15 later   16 honest   17 else   18 mean
19 but   20 into   21 wrong   22 happened   23 dropped
24 want   25 too

Post-listening
4 Ask students why they might write to a problem page. Do they think they are useful? What kind of people use them? In pairs, students match the letters and the people.
Answers: A Iago   B Cassio   C Othello

In their pairs, they can choose one person to write back to. Elicit the language that they might be able to use to give advice: *You should(n't) …, Why don't you …, Think about …, If I were you , I'd …*.

36 Treasure Island (pages 66-67)

Background information: Robert Louis Stevenson was born in Edinburgh in 1850. He died forty-four years later (1894) on a small Samoan island in the Pacific. During his short life he travelled the world and became one of the most famous writers of the 19th century.

Stevenson wrote *Treasure Island* for his stepson in 1881. It is an exciting tale of pirates, buried treasure and danger. It tells the story of young Jim Hawkins and his adventures in the search for the buried treasure of the evil Captain Flint.

Listening aims: Listening for specific information – multiple choice; pronounciation

New vocabulary: treasure, captain, sailor, pirate, island, cook

Pre-listening
1 Discuss what students can see on the map. Let them work in pairs to read the information and solve the puzzle.
Answer: 3

2 Discuss the characters and let them choose who they would like to be in the story and to explain why.

Listening
3 Give students one or two minutes to read the multiple choice questions before listening. Play the recording twice.
Answers: 1A   2B   3C   4B   5C   6C   7A   8C   9B   10C

Post-listening
4 Students discuss the question in small groups or as a class.
5 Let students try to do the exercise without listening to the recording first. Then play the recording through once. Play it again but stop after each word to check the answers.
Answers: 1 measure   2 so   3 night, bite   4 sung
5 note, coat   6 meal   7 nearly   8 lose

1 A Surprise Lunch

1) Work in pairs. Discuss these questions.

a) When did you last eat some fruit?
b) When did you last eat some vegetables?
c) When did you last eat some chocolate?
d) When did you last eat some crisps?
e) What healthy food did you eat yesterday? Make a list.
f) What unhealthy food did you eat yesterday? Make a list.

2) Look at the pictures of Max's and Robbie's lunch boxes. Which lunch box would you prefer? Why?

3) Listen to the first part of the conversation. Read the sentences and tick Yes or No.

	YES	NO
a) Max has the same thing for lunch everyday.		
b) Max thinks his lunch is exciting.		
c) Robbie has different things for lunch.		
d) Robbie is jealous of Max.		
e) Max only likes cheese sandwiches.		
f) Max's mother says he can only have cheese sandwiches.		

4) Look at this picture of Max's brother and read what he says. What do you think he is going to do?

Max always wants something different. I've got an idea.

Listen to the second part of the conversation to find out if you were correct.

TIMESAVER ELEMENTARY LISTENING *have got*

5 🎧 **Listen and draw what's in the lunch boxes.**

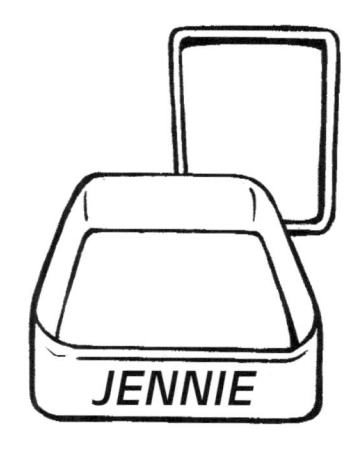

MAX JENNIE ROBBIE

6 **Game. What have you got in your sandwiches? Choose one thing from each column. Your partner will guess what you have got.**

A	B	C
chicken	tomato	salt
cheese	lettuce	pepper
egg	onion	chocolate spread
beef	cucumber	peanut butter

Have you got cheese, tomato and pepper in your sandwich?

I've got tomato and pepper but I haven't got cheese.

Have you got chicken, tomato and pepper?

Yes, I have.

2 Christmas is Coming

1 Find some Christmas words. Match the word halves and label each picture.

a

ang

c

tin

b

ation

tur

key

sel

d

sent

e

er

crack

pre

decor

el

f

2 Will is trying to find out what his Christmas present is. His friend Vicki is helping him. Listen to Part 1 and tick where Vicki and Will look.

behind the wardrobe		under the stairs	
on the wardrobe		behind the fridge	
in his parents' bedroom		behind the sofa	
under the bed		in the lounge	
in the bathroom		under the sofa	

TIMESAVER ELEMENTARY LISTENING prepositions

3 🎧 **Now listen to Part 2 and complete the sentences.**

Dad: Will! What are you (1).......................... ?

Will: Er, looking (2).......................... this, er, beautiful (3).......................... !

Dad: That's good. You can have it (4).......................... Christmas and Uncle Les can have (5).......................... present.

Presenter: Christmas Day

Uncle Les: Happy Christmas, Will. Nice (6).......................... ! I love my new (7)..........................
What a (8).......................... present!

Will: Doh!

4 🎧 **Will's dad is hiding presents before Christmas. Listen and draw the presents in the correct place.**

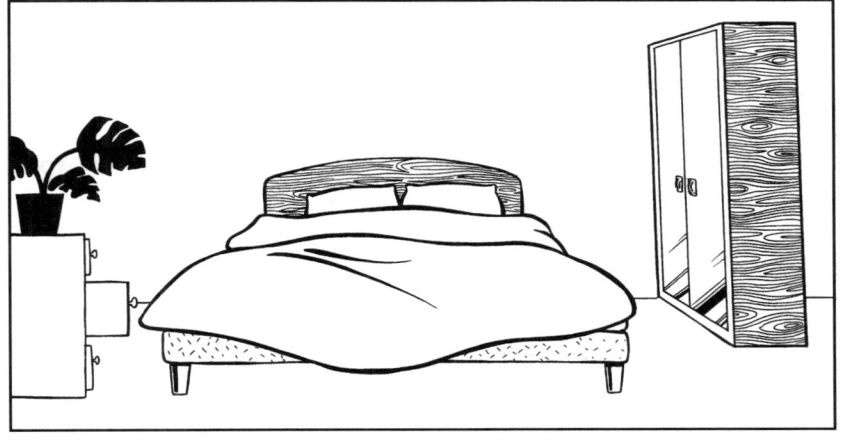

5 **Game. Noughts and Crosses.**

Work in pairs. Make a correct sentence and put a nought or a cross on the grid. The same preposition cannot be used twice in the same game. Listen carefully to each other.

TIMESAVER ELEMENTARY LISTENING feelings / times

3 The Babysitter

1) How do you feel in different situations? Answer these questions then ask a partner.

Do you feel ...	Me	Partner
a) frightened when you see a spider?		
b) bored in some lessons at school?		
c) angry if a friend is late?		
d) happy when you go to the dentist?		
e) sleepy when you have to get up?		
f) hungry after doing a lot of exercise?		

Now make sentences like the examples:

We both feel frightened when we see a spider.
   OR
Neither of us / One of us feels frightened when we see a spider.

2) Max wants to earn some money so he decides to go babysitting. Listen and complete the sentences with one or two words.

a) Max asks his mother for ....
b) Max has to phone Mrs Wilson if he wants to get some ....
c) Mrs Wilson tells Max he can take what .... from the fridge.
d) Mrs Wilson gives Max her .... number.
e) Max gives the child an .... and a ....
f) Max plays .... with the child and .... a book.
g) Mrs Wilson comes back at ....
h) Max is ....

3) Look at the faces. Listen to the feelings and draw the correct face.

4) Listen to Max. Draw the correct times on the clocks.

5) Discuss.

How much pocket money do you get?
Do you have to do anything to get your pocket money?
How do you earn extra pocket money? Do you babysit?
What do you spend your pocket money on?

4 The Maths Test

1 What's the matter? Choose the correct illness. Tick (✓) the box.

1 He's got
a) an ear ache ☐
b) a stomach ache ☐

2 He's got
a) a broken arm ☐
b) a broken toe ☐

3 He's got
a) a stomach ache ☐
b) a cold ☐

4 He's got
a) toothache ☐
b) a headache ☐

5 He's got
a) a cold ☐
b) a broken leg ☐

6 He's got
a) a broken leg ☐
b) a broken heart ☐

2 Listen to Will's story and tick (✓) Yes or No.

	YES	NO
a) The date is Thursday the 6th.		
b) Will likes maths.		
c) Will says he feels unwell.		
d) Will wants to see the doctor.		
e) The doctor gives Will some chocolate.		
f) Will has to take his medicine three times a day.		
g) Mum tells Will he can return to school the next day.		
h) The maths teacher isn't well.		
i) Will will have to do the maths test on Wednesday.		

3 Who says these sentences – Will, his mother or the doctor? Listen again and write W, M or D.

a) Are you all right, dear? ....
b) What's the matter, Will? ....
c) Ouch, it hurts. ....
d) This is serious. ....
e) It's ten to nine already. ....
f) Thank you, doctor. ....

4 Are you good at thinking up excuses? Look at these ones and add one of your own. Work with a partner.

1 Where is your homework?
a) The dog ate it.
b) I left it on the bus.
c) A bully took it out of my bag and threw it in the river.
d) ....

2 Why are you late?
a) My mother's car had a flat tyre on the way to school.
b) I helped an old lady across the road and carried her bags home for her.
c) I forgot my PE kit so I had to run home for it.
d) ....

3 Why aren't you in class?
a) I thought it was lunch time.
b) I'm taking a message to the maths teacher.
c) I'm looking for Charlie. He isn't in class.
d) ....

Now choose one of the situations and excuses. Role play being a teacher and student.

5 Will's T-shirt

1 What would you wear to a party? Think about the accessories too.

2 Listen to the story of Will's T-shirt. Choose the correct answers, A, B or C.

1 Which is Will's T-shirt?

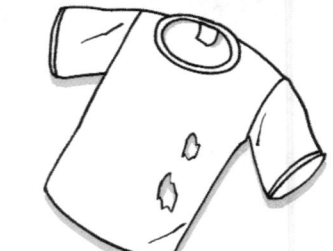

A B C

2 How much does Will's mother give him?

A £10.00 B £5.00 C £75.00

3 Which is the second shop Will goes to?

A Charity Shop B Sports Supplies C Department Store

TIMESAVER ELEMENTARY LISTENING *too*

4 What's wrong with the first T-shirt Will tries on?

A ☐   B ☐   C ☐

5 What did Will buy?

A ☐   B ☐   C ☐

6 How did Will's Mum feel?

A ☐   B ☐   C ☐

3 Look at the picture. Find seven problems.

a *The hat is too big.*

6 Vicki's Pet

1 Find the mystery pet. Write the letters in the boxes. Would you like to own the mystery pet?

TIMESAVER ELEMENTARY LISTENING embedded questions

2 🎧 **Vicki wants Will to look after her hamster while she is on holiday. Listen and put the pictures in the correct order.**

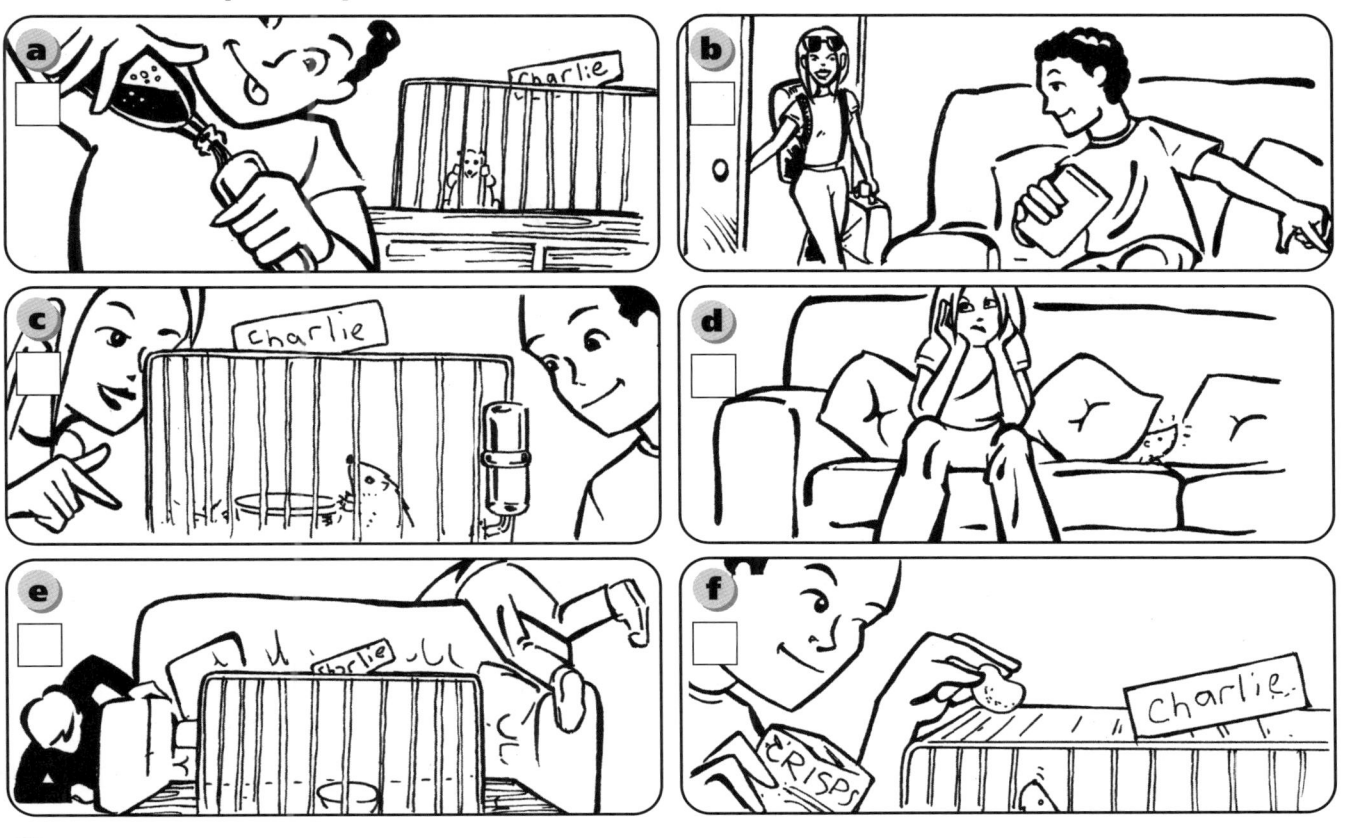

a)
b)
c)
d)
e)
f)

3 Read this example from the story.

I don't know how you can live in that cage.

There is a question in that sentence:

How can you live in the cage?

We have added *I don't know*. What happens to the word order?

Add *I don't know* to the beginning of these questions.

a) How can you drink only water?
....

b) How can you eat that disgusting food?
....

c) What time is it?
....

d) Where is Charlie?
....

e) How much is the new Linkin Park CD?
....

f) Where was Vicki yesterday?
....

g) Why isn't Will here?
....

h) What is Vicki's favourite film?
....

7 Travelling by Train

1 Put the words in the correct part of the Venn diagram.

conductor
single ticket   pilot
return ticket
ticket office   seatbelt
driver   tracks   seat
to take off   to get on
engine   runway
steward   guard
to land   to get off
platform

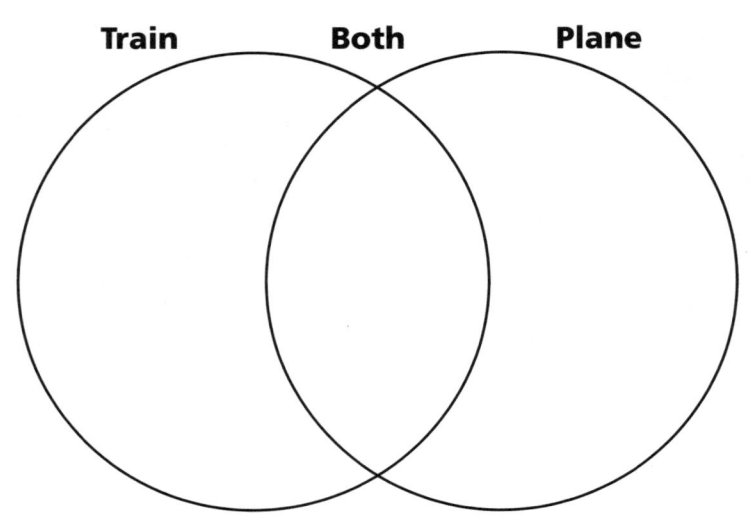

Train   Both   Plane

2 This story is about a trip Will makes. Listen to Part 1 and complete the sentences.

a) Will wants to go .... with his friends.

b) Mum suggests he ....

c) Will takes .... to his aunty.

d) Will thinks the train journey is .... and ....

e) Will feels .... when he sees his friends.

f) At the train station, Will asks for .... to Forest Hill.

g) Will pays ....

3 Listen to Part 2. Will is at his aunt's house. Read the sentences and tick Yes or No.

	YES	NO
a) Mum says Will can't go skateboarding.		
b) His aunt agrees with his mother.		
c) Uncle Tom is too old to skateboard.		
d) Will thinks his uncle is quite good at skateboarding.		
e) Uncle Tom only wants one turn at skateboarding.		

4 Read the jumbled dialogue at the train station. Listen and put the sentences in order.

- GOODBYE!
- HELLO. A TICKET TO FOREST HILL, PLEASE.
- YES I'M TWELVE.
- HERE'S THE CHANGE AND YOUR TICKET.
- THEN YOU CAN HAVE A CHILD'S TICKET.
- ONE CHILD RETURN TO FOREST HILL. THAT'S £3.20
- ARE YOU UNDER SIXTEEN?
- SINGLE OR RETURN?
- HERE'S FIVE POUNDS.
- HOW MUCH IS IT?
- RETURN PLEASE.

5 Write about a journey you have been on. Answer the questions to help you.

Where did you go?
Who did you go with?
How did you go?
Was the journey interesting or boring? Why?
Did you arrive on time or were you late?

8 Lucky Socks

1 Which of these is lucky and which is unlucky?

2 Listen to the story of Will and his lucky socks and put the sentences in the correct order.

a) A teacher sees Will with no socks on. ☐
b) A teacher tells Will to take his socks off. ☐
c) Will gets a detention. ☐
d) Will is late for his football match. ☐
e) Will gets a detention. ☐
f) The other football team laugh at Will's socks. ☐
g) Will gets a detention. ☐
h) Will's team score a goal. ☐
i) Vicki gets a detention. ☐
j) Will is late for school. ☐
k) Will is wearing green socks. ☐
l) Will has to write lines. ☐

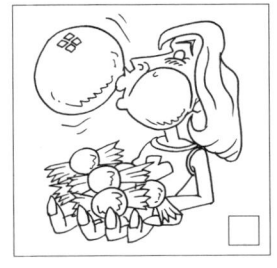

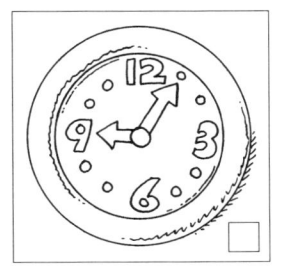

3 Will doesn't like his school rules so he has decided to write some new ones. Tick (✔) the things you must do and cross (✘) the things you mustn't do.

4 Write your own school rules. Write three things you *must do* and three things you *mustn't do*.

....
....
....

TIMESAVER ELEMENTARY LISTENING — I'd like / I like

9 Eating Out

1) Work out the flavours of the different ice creams.

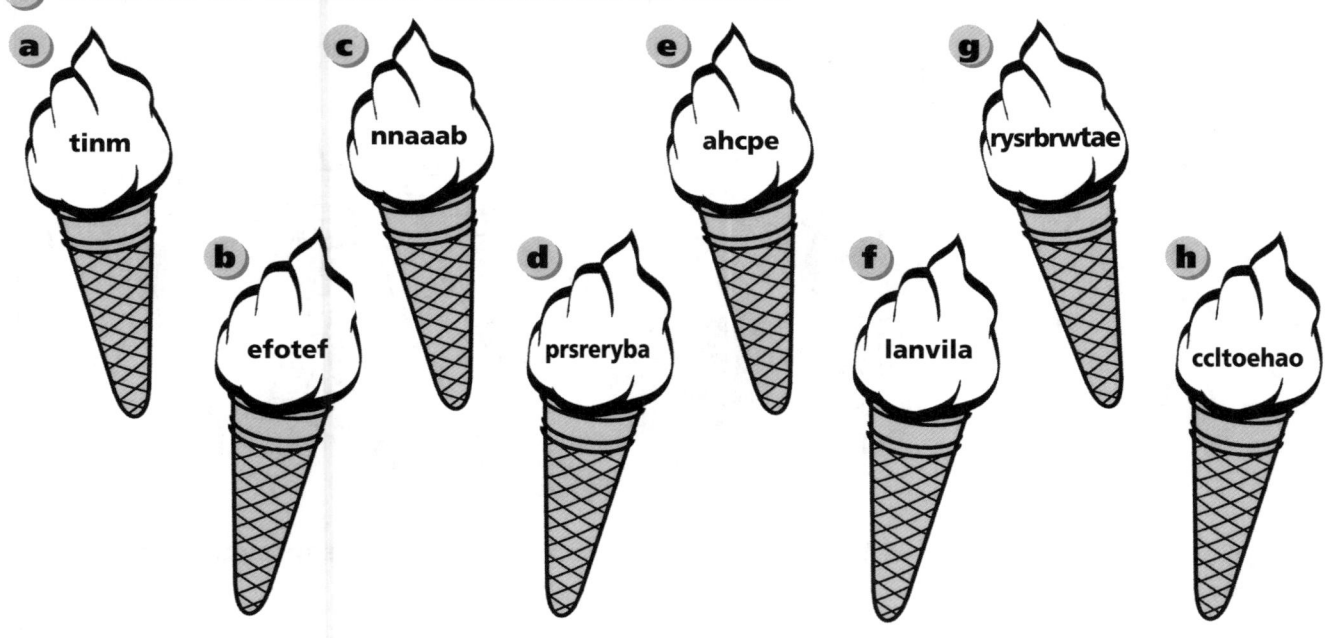

a) tinm
b) efotef
c) nnaaab
d) prsreryba
e) ahcpe
f) lanvila
g) rysrbrwtae
h) ccltoehao

2) 🎧 1/18 **David and Victoria are in a restaurant in Italy. Look at the menu. What would they like to eat? Write D for David and V for Victoria.**

Starters
- Green salad ☐
- Tomato salad ☐
- Melon ☐

Main course
- Fish ☐
- Steak ☐
- Pizza Margerita ☐
- Four cheese pizza ☐
- Pepperoni pizza ☐

Dessert
- Apple pie ☐
- Ice cream ☐
- Chocolate cake ☐

3) 🎧 1/19 **Listen and tick the sentences you hear.**

1. a) I'd like fish. ☐
   b) I like fish. ☐

2. a) I'd like chicken. ☐
   b) I like chicken. ☐

3. a) Would you like chocolate ice cream? ☐
   b) Do you like chocolate ice cream? ☐

4. a) What would you like? ☐
   b) What do you like? ☐

4) Work in small groups. Create your own menu with your favourite foods. Follow the menu in Exercise 2.

Swap your menu with another group. One of you is the waiter. Take the orders from the rest of your group.

TIMESAVER ELEMENTARY LISTENING — I'd like / I like

5 🔊 **Listen to The Bubble Gum Rap without looking at the words. Tick (✓) the pictures of the flavours you hear.**

--- THE BUBBLEGUM RAP ---

I like strawberry, cherry
Cola too
Can be pink and can be blue
I don't care
It's no trouble
I just wanna blow that bubble

Chew with me
Chew and tap
That's the name of the bubble gum rap.

I've got banana, blueberry
Lemon and lime
Chew together

They'll turn to slime
Oh I don't care
It's no trouble
I just wanna blow that bubble.

It's sticky, it's like glue
Open up and
Start to chew
I don't care
It's no trouble
I just wanna blow that bubble

Chew with me
Chew and tap
You can do the bubble gum rap

Yep, I really love
My bubble gum
Not in school or
In front of Mum
But I make certain
I am sure
I put it in the bin
And not on the floor!

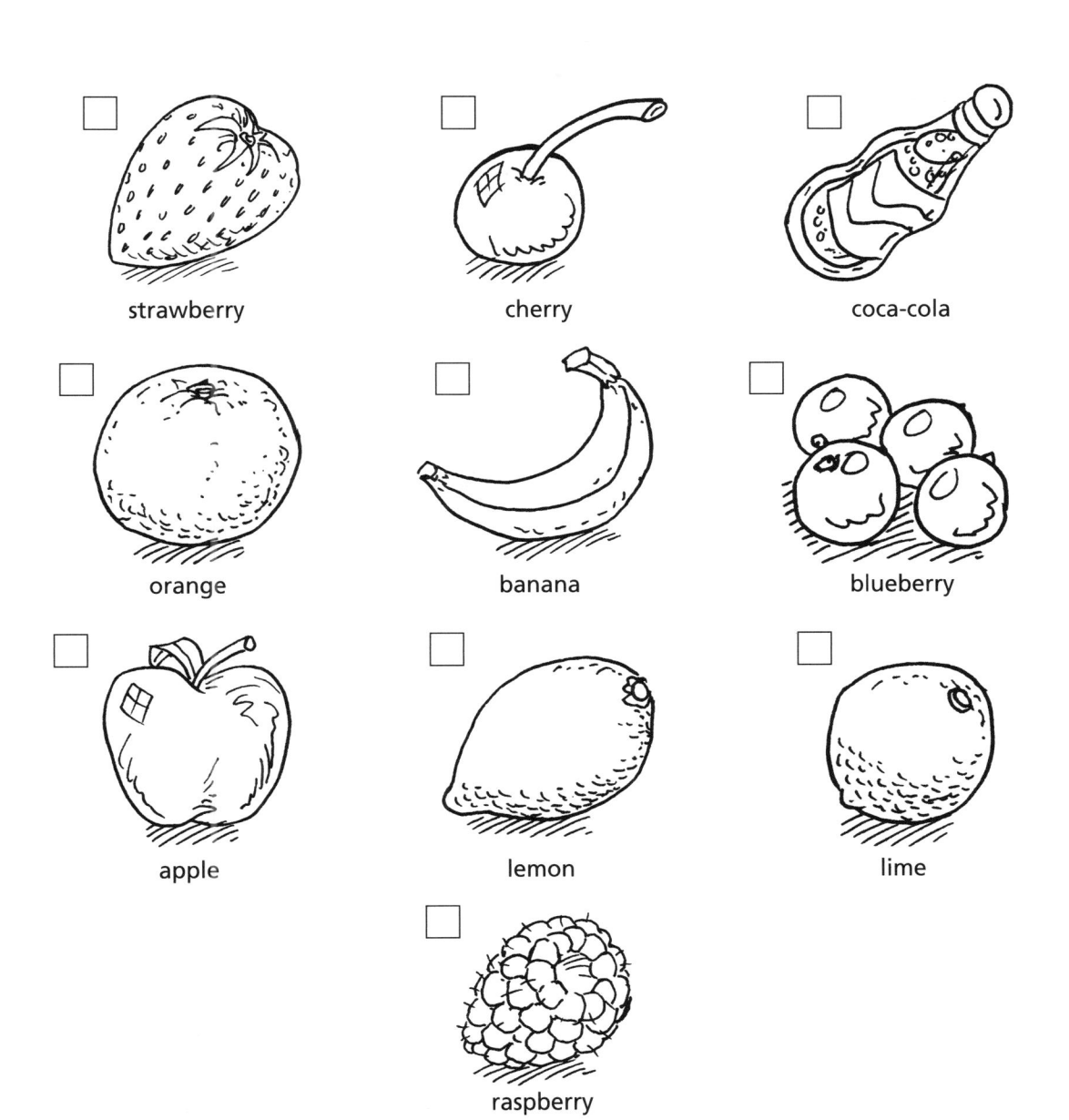

☐ strawberry   ☐ cherry   ☐ coca-cola

☐ orange   ☐ banana   ☐ blueberry

☐ apple   ☐ lemon   ☐ lime

☐ raspberry

TIMESAVER ELEMENTARY LISTENING *going to*

10 Summer Holidays

1 Look at the photos from a theme park. Which two rides would you like to go on?

2 🔊 Max and Robbie are in Brighton. They are at a funfair. Listen and tick the correct pictures.

TIMESAVER ELEMENTARY LISTENING *going to*

5 a ☐   b ☐

6 a ☐   b ☐

3 🎧 1.22 **Listen to what Max is going to do in the holidays. Write the correct day under each picture.**

a   b   c   d

....

e   f   g

....

4 🎧 1.23 **Listen and tick what David is going to take to the beach.**

Sunglasses ☐
Sun hat ☐
Parasol ☐
CD player ☐
Swimming trunks ☐
Camera ☐
Flip flops ☐
Towel ☐
Sun oil ☐

5 **Look at the things David is going to take. Add five things of your own.**

Work in pairs. Show your partner your list. You can take only seven things with you in total.

TIMESAVER ELEMENTARY LISTENING   shapes / like

11 The Mystery Picture

1 How many examples of each shape can you find?

2 Listen and draw the picture.

3 What do the pictures look like?

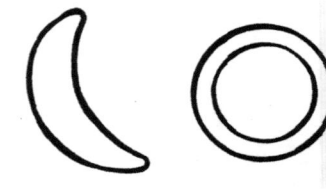

It looks like a moon.

4 Answer these questions.

a) What kind of food do you like?
....

b) What's the weather like in May?
....

c) What is your head teacher like?
....

d) Who do you look like?
....

e) Do you like exercises like this?
....

TIMESAVER ELEMENTARY LISTENING adverbs of frequency

12 American Festivals

1) Discuss in pairs.

What festivals do you have in your country? Which is your favourite?
Do you dress up or wear special clothes? Do you give presents?
Do you eat special food? Do you have a party?
Do you get time off school?

2) 🎧 **Listen to the people talking about American festivals. Match each person with the festival they are talking about.**

Speaker 1	Vicky	New Year's Day
Speaker 2	Jeanette	Independence Day
Speaker 3	Alex	Halloween
Speaker 4	Adam	Thanksgiving

3) 🎧 **Listen again. Match the festivals with each sentence. Write N (New Year's Day), ID (Independence Day), H (Halloween) or T (Thanksgiving).**

a) Children really like this festival. ....
b) People make promises. ....
c) This is in November. ....
d) Children dress up. ....
e) People try to give up bad habits. ....
f) People go to church. ....
g) Children are given nice things to eat. ....
h) People see relatives they haven't seen for a while. ....
i) People have barbecues and picnics with their families. ....
j) People put a vegetable outside their house. ....
k) People eat turkey. ....
l) People watch firework displays in the evening. ....
m) Americans feel pleased to be American. ....

4) Choose the correct words and find another day which Americans celebrate.

a) This day *is always* (L) / *always is* (S) the first Monday in September.
b) People *have usually* (T) / *usually have* (A) a day off work.
c) People *go sometimes* (A) / *sometimes go* (B) to a country fair.
d) There *are often* (O) / *often are* (T) parades in towns.
e) The President *speaks always* (E) / *always speaks* (R) to the people.

The celebration is .... Day.

TIMESAVER ELEMENTARY LISTENING   prefer

13 England vs America

1 Write down three adjectives which you think describe the United States and three which describe Britain.

United States: ....

Britain: ....

2 🎧 Listen to the kids from Phoenix School. What do they say about England and what do they say about America. Write the words after the correct country.

| too big   too small   amazing   dangerous   exciting   safe   boring |

United States: ....

Britain: ....

3 Look at the pictures and ask your partner questions like the examples.

a *Do you prefer America or England?* UK USA *I like America, but I prefer England. I think America is too big.*

b *Do you prefer eating fruit or hamburgers for lunch usually?*

c

d

e

f

4 Read this postcard from Dave to Jane. What could you write instead of 'cool'?

> Hi Jane
> Here I am in New York. What a cool place! I'm staying with my aunt and uncle – they have a really cool house with a swimming pool in the back garden. The people I've met here are really cool too – they all love my accent. My cousins took me to a very cool restaurant last night. The food was so cool and you could eat as much as you wanted. I felt a bit ill afterwards! Tomorrow we're going up the Empire State Building and then shopping – that'll be cool.
> Back next week.
>
> Love Dave xxx

14 India

1 What do you know about India? Match the definitions in column A with the words in column B.

A	B
1 the most popular Indian food	a) Taj Mahal
2 the most famous Indian building	b) Mumbai
3 the most common religion	c) Mahatma Gandhi
4 the largest city in India	d) chess
5 the most famous Indian person	e) yoga
6 one of the most difficult games, invented in India	f) curry
7 one of the oldest forms of exercise	g) Hinduism

2 Listen to the conversation about India and find out why these numbers are said.

a) 12 million ....

b) 900 million ....

c) 1600 ....

d) thousands ....

3 Listen again. Are the following sentences True or False?

a) Mount Everest is in India. ....

b) More people live in India than China. ....

c) English is the official language. ....

d) There are more than 1600 languages in India. ....

e) There are no tigers in India now. ....

f) Everyone in India has clean water. ....

g) The film making industry is very important in India. ....

4 Work in pairs. Compare your country with India. Use the words in the box.

> big   poor   hot   expensive   modern

Is your country bigger than India?

No, I think it's smaller.

Then ask about the following:

> high mountains   busy cities   size of population   number of languages

Are the mountains in your country higher than in India?

No, I don't think they are as high.

TIMESAVER ELEMENTARY LISTENING suggestions and excuses

15 What Shall We Do?

1) Work in groups of eight. Find out what people in your class do after school.

	Yes	No
Hang out with friends		
Do homework		
Go to a club		
Do a hobby		
Do a sport		
Watch TV		
Play on the computer		
Work		

2) Listen to Adam and Jennifer talking about what they're going to do after school. Adam has lots of suggestions, but there is always a problem. For each suggestion, circle the problem that Jennifer talks about.

Suggestion	Problem	
1 play a computer game	a) The computer doesn't work.	**b) Computer games are boring.** (circled)
2 go swimming	a) The water's always too cold.	b) I can't swim.
3 go skateboarding	a) Skateboarding is for boys.	b) It's too difficult.
4 go to the cinema	a) I haven't got enough money.	b) There aren't any good films.
5 go to the Internet café	a) The Internet café is too far away.	b) We did that yesterday.

What does Jennifer want to do after school? ....

3) Listen again and complete the sentences.

1 .... to my house?
2 .... swimming.
3 .... skateboarding?
4 .... to the cinema, then?
5 .... to the Internet café?

4) Work in groups of three. You're trying to find a new hobby you can all do. First think up a second excuse for each activity. Then have the conversation. Take turns at suggesting activities. Then think of a new hobby you could all do.

Suggestion	Excuse 1	Excuse 2
ballet	I don't like wearing pink.	
yoga	It's boring.	
rugby	It's too dangerous	
in-line hockey	I'm not fit enough.	
go-karting	It's too expensive.	

Student A: Let's do ballet.
Student B: No, I don't like wearing pink.
Student C: And I don't like the music.

16 A Phone Call from Jamaica

1 Solve these anagrams to find different kinds of holidays. There are some clues below to help you. One does not have a picture – which one is it?

a) scieru ....

b) nicpmga ....

c) gisikn ....

d) gkpceaa ....

e) naliisg ....

f) ctvatyii ....

g) knlwaig ....

h) nyoomhnoe ....

2 Listen to the phone call between Jennifer and Kate and look at the holiday pictures. Tick (✓) the one in each pair which is correct.

1a ☐   1b ☐   2a ☐   2b ☐   3a ☐   3b ☐

3 Listen again and complete these sentences.

Kate: Are you enjoying (1).................... ?

Jennifer: We're all enjoying (2).................... very much.

Jennifer: Dad burnt (3).................... while he was sunbathing yesterday.

Jennifer: Mum bought (4).................... a reggae CD and now Mum and Dad are trying to teach (5).................... a Jamaican dance.

Jennifer: The next time we see (6).................... we'll be at school.

Kate: All my friends are on holiday, but I'm at home by (7).................... .

4 Tick the sentence if it is correct. Remove the reflexive pronoun if it is not necessary.

a) I get myself up at 7a.m. each morning. ....

b) My little brother and sister wake themselves up at 7.30. ....

c) I usually make myself breakfast because my mother is too busy. ....

d) I have myself a shower at 7.30. ....

e) I get dressed myself after my shower. ....

f) Everyday before I go to school, my mother says 'Behave yourself!' ....

g) At school we help ourselves to the food at lunchtime – nobody serves us. ....

h) My younger brother fell over in the playground yesterday and hurt himself quite badly. ....

i) I go myself to sleep at about 10 o'clock. ....

j) I usually dream myself. ....

17 Valentine's Day

1) Would you give someone you liked any of these presents on Valentine's Day? Why?/ Why not?

2) Listen to Kate and Simon talking about Valentine's Day and tick the correct answer.

	Kate	Simon
a) Who likes Valentine's Day?		
b) Who thinks it is a waste of money?		
c) Who has a Valentine's card?		
d) Who doesn't want to show their card?		
e) Who knows the sender?		
f) Who wrote the card?		
g) Who is lying?		
h) Who knows a secret?		

TIMESAVER ELEMENTARY LISTENING question tags

3 🎧 1/30 **Listen again and complete the sentences with the correct question tags.**

> isn't it?   are you?   didn't you?   do you?   doesn't it?   did you?

Kate: I love Valentine's Day – getting a card from someone who likes you. It always makes you happy, (1)............................ .

Simon: I don't think so. I think it's silly. Everyone wastes their money on cards and then they don't write their names in them, so you don't know who your card is from.

Kate: Yes, but having a secret card is really exciting, (2)............................ .

Simon: No, it's stupid.

Kate: Oh, I see. You didn't get a Valentine's card from anyone, (3)............................

Simon: Yes, I did.

Kate: Well, where is it?

Simon: It's in my bag, but you don't really want to see it, (4)............................

Kate: Of course I do! I know all the girls in your class. I can tell you who it's from.

Simon: OK, here it is.

Kate: *To my wonderful Simon, You're so handsome and so clever. I think I'm going to love you forever* – I know this writing. You wrote this card, (5)............................

Simon: No, I didn't.

Kate: I know that you're lying. Your face is red.

Simon: OK, you're right, but you're not going to tell anyone, (6)............................

Kate: Let me think … not if you help me with my maths homework and lend me your stereo and buy me some chocolate and …

4 🎧 1/31 **Listen to the sentences with question tags again and repeat them. Remember: If your voice goes down, you're asking someone to agree with you. If your voice goes up, you're asking someone a question. Which ones ask a question?**

5 **Work with a partner. In the middle box, complete the sentences with information about your partner. In the last box, write in the correct question tag.**

1	You are	fourteen,	aren't you?
2	You have		
3	You like		
4	Your father is		
5	Your mother has		
6	You went		
7	You didn't		
8	You aren't		

For example: *You are fourteen, aren't you?*

Now practise each one with your partner. Remember to use the correct intonation. Your partner should answer.

Example:

You are fourteen, aren't you? — Yes, that's right.

You are fourteen, aren't you? — No, I'm thirteen.

TIMESAVER ELEMENTARY LISTENING | joining words

18 Guy Fawkes

1 When do you have fireworks in your country? Discuss. Do you have them at these times – birthdays, weddings, New Year, religious festivals?

2 Listen to the story and put the pictures in the correct order.

3 Listen again and join these sentences. You need to add a word each time and you might have to remove one.

a) Guy Fawkes was a Catholic. He hated the King.

....

b) Guy Fawkes joined a group of men. They wanted to kill the king.

....

c) One of the men had a relative. He often visited the Houses of Parliament.

....

d) He warned his relative about the plan. His relative warned King James.

....

e) Guy Fawkes entered the cellar on the night of November 5th. The King's men were already there.

....

f) They wanted to know the names of the other men. They tortured Guy Fawkes until he confessed.

....

TIMESAVER ELEMENTARY LISTENING joining words

4) Now join these sentences with the words in the box.

| and   so   when   who |

a) Guy Fawkes was a Catholic .... was born in York.

b) The Catholics were not happy .... they decided to blow up Parliament.

c) The King was James V1 of Scotland .... James 1 of England.

d) .... the King found out about the Gunpowder Plot, he told his men to search the cellars.

e) .... the King's men searched the cellars, they found 36 barrels of gunpowder.

f) The leader of the gang was Robert Catesby .... was executed with Guy Fawkes.

g) The conspirators were tortured .... then they were hanged.

h) The Gunpowder Plot failed .... England stayed as a Protestant country.

5) Match the questions and answers and write the capital letters in the box below. They will tell you the name of the man who stopped the conspiracy.

1 Who was King in 1605?

2 Why did Guy Fawkes want to kill the King?

3 What religion was Guy Fawkes?

4 Where did they put the gunpowder?

5 When did they plan to light the gunpowder?

6 Who was in the cellar when Guy Fawkes went in?

7 What did the King's men do to Guy Fawkes?

8 Did Guy Fawkes tell the King's men his friend's name?

9 What finally happened to Guy Fawkes and his friends?

a) Catholic (N)

b) The King's men killed them. (E)

c) Yes, he did. (L)

d) Because he was unfair to Catholics. (O)

e) On November 5th. (E)

f) They tortured him. (G)

g) James. (M)

h) The King's men. (A)

i) In a cellar under the Houses of Parliament. (T)

The name of the man was: Lord [_ _ _ _ _ _ _ _]

19 Holiday Plans

1) Where are these people going on holiday?

a) I'll visit the Taj Mahal and eat some delicious curries. .... *India* ....

b) I'll go to the floating market, visit the Grand Palace and eat very spicy food. ....

c) I'll walk along the Great Wall and go to see the soldiers at Xian. ....

d) I'll climb Table Mountain and spend some time on the beach too. ....

e) I'm looking forward to visiting the different art galleries, going down the canals in a gondola and seeing the Colosseum. ....

f) I'm looking forward to seeing where the Olympics first started. ....

2) Where are Paul and Sally thinking of going on holiday this year? Put the words into the correct boxes.

India   America   Scotland   Ireland   Australia   England

Paul	Sally Ann

3) Perhaps Paul and Sally Ann won't be able to go on holiday. Read the sentences then listen and put a 'P' if the problem is Paul's or an 'S' if the problem is Sally Ann's.

a) Perhaps I won't save enough money. ☐

b) Perhaps my brother won't invite me to his house. ☐

c) Perhaps I won't be able to take a month off work. ☐

d) Perhaps the weather won't be nice. ☐

Now write sentences about Paul and Sally Ann.

If Sally Ann doesn't have enough money, she won't go to America.

4) Tom is going to visit his uncle in America for a holiday. Then he is going to drive around the States with his cousin. His mum is worried about him. Imagine you are Tom. What do you say to your mother?

a) What will you do if you lose your passport?

   If I lose my passport, I will go to the Embassy.

b) What will you do if you are ill?

   ....

c) What will you do if someone steals your money?

   ....

d) What will you do if you can't find a hotel to stay in?

....

e) What will you do if your car breaks down?

....

f) What will you do if you miss your plane home?

....

5 🎧 **Listen to the song and fill the gaps with the correct forms of the verbs in the box.**

> to sit   to spend   to end   to come   to have   to be   to catch   to travel   to relax

--- MY NEW ORLEANS DREAM ---

I'm going to a special place with all of my friends

Down in Louisianan where the Mississippi (1).......................... .

Gonna stay up all night and (2).......................... all day.

Down in my favourite city in the USA.

Chorus

I'm dreaming my New Orleans dream

Old time riverboats powered by steam

Jazz on the streets and houses from the past

I'm dreaming my New Orleans dream

Sunny cafes with coffee and cream

Pack your bags fast – we're going there at last.

We're gonna (3).......................... the summer far away from school.

We're going on vacation. It'll be so cool.

We'll (4).......................... the plane tomorrow. I just can't wait to go

And once we get to New Orleans we won't want to (5).......................... home.

(Chorus)

Where are the flowers? Where are the trees?

Where are the boats that (6).......................... down to the sea?

Where is the music and the warm summer breeze?

Come to New Orleans please.

We can catch a steamboat, we can (7).......................... in the sun

Down by the Mississippi we'll be (8).......................... so much fun

There's singing and there's laughing, there's excitement everywhere

The streets (9).......................... full of people and there's music in the air.

20 Global Warming

1 How green are you? Try this questionnaire.

	Yes, I have.	No, I haven't.
Have you ever …		
1 taken your paper, bottles and cans for recycling?	☐	☐
2 made a compost heap from organic waste?	☐	☐
3 left your computer on when you are not using it?	☐	☐
4 looked for information on eco-issues on the web?	☐	☐
5 asked your parents to drive you less than a kilometre to school or to a friend's house?	☐	☐
6 used your bicycle or walked instead of going by car?	☐	☐
7 dropped litter in the street?	☐	☐
8 used a tumble dryer when it's not raining?	☐	☐
9 left the tap on when you are brushing your teeth?	☐	☐
10 given your old clothes to a charity shop?	☐	☐
11 planted a tree?	☐	☐
12 cleaned up an area in your neighbourhood?	☐	☐

Check your answers below. Who is the greenest in the class?

2 Listen and tick the words you hear.

temperatures ☐   sea level ☐   globe ☐   degrees ☐   rice ☐   air ☐
hot ☐   flooded ☐   pollution ☐   warm ☐   villages ☐   rainforest ☐

3 Listen again. Are the sentences below True or False? Write T or F in the boxes.

a) The world will be five degrees warmer by the end of this century. ☐
b) 1996 was the hottest year on record. ☐
c) By 2080, 25% of all coastal towns will be flooded. ☐
d) Most carbon dioxide comes from factories, homes and cars. ☐
e) Trees absorb oxygen. ☐

4 Read these comments then correct them using *unless*.

We don't need to do anything about global warming. The sea level won't rise.

No. Unless we do something about global warming, the sea level will rise.

a) We don't need to save fuel. There will be enough for the future.

b) We don't need to protect our lakes and rivers. They won't become polluted.

c) We don't need to stop cutting down rainforests. The hole in the ozone layer won't get bigger.

d) We don't need to stop global warming. Temperatures won't rise further.

5 In groups, think of three things you could do to help stop global warming. Listen to the other groups and choose the best five suggestions.

Key: Get 1 point if you said YES to questions 1, 2, 4, 6, 10, 11, 12. Get 1 point if you said NO to questions 3, 5, 7, 8, 9. The more points you get, the greener you are.

21 What's your school like?

1 Read the description and label the rooms on the plan of the school.

As you come into the school, you will see the reception on the left. This is where the headmaster's secretary and assistant sit. The headmaster's room is behind that. If you go left after the reception you will find two English classrooms opposite each other. Next to one of the English classrooms, on the left, is the drama room. Opposite that is a History classroom.

Now turn around and go straight on until you come to another classroom on your right. This is the Geography classroom. There is a maths classroom opposite it and beside it there is a music room.

Turn around again and go back and turn right. On your right, the large room is the hall where we have assemblies and other meetings. Diagonally across from the hall is the Dining Room. They serve quite good lunches there. What's the food like at your school?

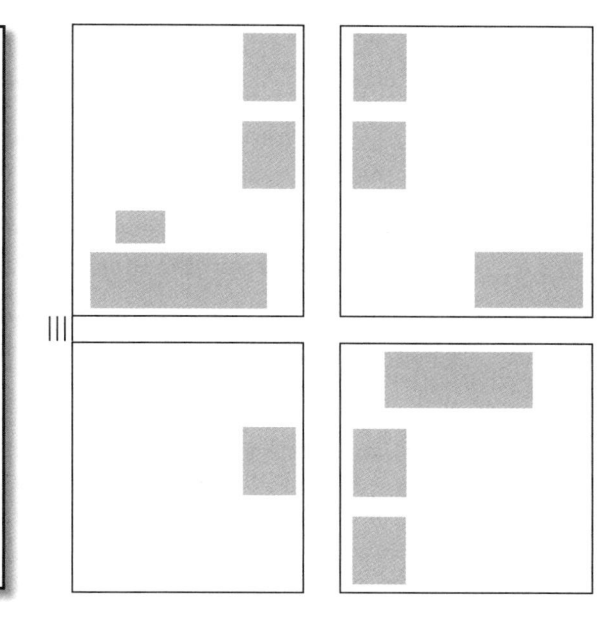

2 Listen to Kate, Simon, Adam and Jennifer talking about their schools and then complete the chart.

	Kate	Simon	Adam	Jennifer
Do you like going to school?		yes		
What do you like best about school?			sport	
What's the worst thing about school?	homework			
What are your teachers like?				friendly

3 Put the words in brackets in the correct place.

a) I like going to school. (very much) .... *I like going to school very much.* ....

b) I don't like science. (at all) ....

c) The subject I like is biology. (best) ....

d) I enjoy sport. (always) ....

e) I don't like my other lessons. (any of) ....

f) My lessons are interesting. (most of) ....

4 Complete these sentences about yourself.

a) The best thing about my school is ....

b) The worst thing about my school is ....

c) At school I am good at ....

d) At school I am bad at ....

5 Which would you choose – to be educated at home or to be educated at school? In groups, think of arguments for and against your choice. Present them to the class and then take a vote on the best method.

TIMESAVER ELEMENTARY LISTENING | discussion – American High School

22 Beverly Hills High School

1 Find the complete words about American schools in the word search.

a) A g _ _ _ _ is the American word for a school year group.

b) A s _ _ _ _ _ _ _ _ is the American word meaning 'term'.

c) A p _ _ _ is a party that students go to when they finish their last year at school.

d) A y _ _ _ _ _ _ _ is a school diary with photographs and information about the students.

e) A f _ _ _ _ _ _ _ _ is a first year student at an American High School.

f) A s _ _ _ _ _ _ _ _ _ is a second year student at an American High School.

```
S O P H O M O R E
K I R D S G O F T
E K O O B R A E Y
N B M E C A O M E
V E R Y F D A M O
U R E T S E M E S
S F R E S H M A N
```

You are going to listen to two people talking about Beverly Hills High School. Most of the kids who go there come from rich families. There's a television show about it too. The letters left in the word search will tell you what happens to some students at this school. Write the sentence below.

....

2 Listen to the people talking about the school. What do these numbers refer to?

2000 ....   45 ....

96 ....   118 ....

58 ....   34 ....

25 ....

3 Read these facts about the school.

Beverly Hills High School is the most glamorous school in America.

The school has two theatres, a TV studio and a school radio station.

Lots of the kids at the school drive themselves to school when they reach 16. Some of them have Porsches, BMWs and Jeeps.

Students with cars have to pay $250 a term to park their car in the school car park.

Now add three more facts from the listening.

....

....

....

4 Discussion. Would you like to go to this school? What are the advantages and disadvantages?

23 Coral Reefs

1 Where is the biggest coral reef? Test your knowledge about coral reefs by choosing True or False and find out.

		True	False
a)	You can see coral reefs from space.	A	G
b)	You can put coral in food to make it taste salty.	R	U
c)	One quarter of all the plants that live in the sea, grow in coral reefs.	S	E
d)	It takes millions of tiny animals to make a coral reef.	T	E
e)	Coral reefs need deep water.	N	R
f)	A coral reef doesn't protect the coast from damage by storms.	L	A
g)	Doctors can use medicine from coral to mend broken bones.	L	A
h)	Hurricanes damage coral reefs more than people.	I	N
i)	If we damage the reefs, there won't be enough food for the fish.	A	D

2 Read the sentences below. What does Mrs Kingsley say we must and mustn't do to protect the reefs? Tick (✔) the sentences.

a) We must keep the reefs clean. ☐
b) We must grow more plants on the coral reefs. ☐
c) We must stop putting rubbish in the sea. ☐
d) We mustn't visit coral reefs. ☐
e) We mustn't disturb the water around the reefs. ☐
f) We mustn't photograph the reefs. ☐

3 Look at the example from the listening. Use the verbs in the box to complete the other sentences.

> ~~disappear~~   cut down   think   get   become   damage

a) Coral reefs _are disappearing_.
b) Our cities .... more polluted.
c) People .... forests.
d) People .... the countryside.
e) People .... more about the environment.
f) Fuel .... more expensive.

4 In groups, discuss the sentences in exercise 3. Which of these things are good? Which are bad? What do you think we should be doing?

TIMESAVER ELEMENTARY LISTENING | discussion – countries

24 An Interesting Country

1 Look at the pictures. What do they have in common?

2 Listen to the conversation about Scotland and then match the sentence halves below.

1 Robert Burns is the poet
2 Bagpipes are instruments
3 Haggis is a kind of sausage
4 Kilts are men's clothes
5 Alexander Graham Bell was the man
6 Robert Louis Stevenson was the writer
7 The Loch Ness Monster is the strange animal
8 The Highland Fling is a dance

a) who was famous for writing *Jekyll and Hyde* and *Treasure Island*.
b) that is made from meat and animal fat.
c) that are made from tartan.
d) that Scottish people play on special occasions.
e) that lives in a lake.
f) that is very lively and popular in Scotland.
g) who people remember every year on Burns' Night.
h) who invented the telephone.

3 Scotland is famous for the Loch Ness Monster and whisky. Look at these pictures. Which countries do they represent? Work in pairs. Ask the question and add to the list.

a) *What is Italy famous for?* It's famous for pizzas ... and pasta ...

b) ....

c) ....

TIMESAVER ELEMENTARY LISTENING discussion – countries

d) ....

e) ....

f) ....

4 🎧 **Listen to the conversation between Rebecca and Steve. Match the beginning of the suggestions they make with the correct endings.**

1 Shall we   a) go out for a meal?
2 Let's not   b) buy some turnips and potatoes.
3 Let's   c) have a haggis.
4 Why don't we   d) going to see the fireworks?
5 How about   e) make our own haggis or buy one?

5 Are the following kinds of food countable or uncountable? Put them in the correct box. Some of them can be countable and uncountable. Why?

haggis   turnip   meat   potato   animal fat   vegetable   beef   chicken

countable	both	uncountable

6 Imagine you have been asked to prepare a poster to encourage people to visit your country. Work in groups and decide what you would include and then prepare your poster to present to the rest of the class.

TIMESAVER ELEMENTARY LISTENING | discussion – stereotypes

25 A Typical English Person

1 What do you know about England? Look at the headings and discuss them with a partner.

- Food
- Sport
- Places
- People
- Weather

2 Listen to Tom and Helen talking about English customs. Complete the chart by circling the things they choose.

	Tom	Helen
drinks	tea / ~~coffee~~	tea / ~~coffee~~
eats	fish and chips / curry	fish and chips / curry
favourite sport	football / tennis	football / tennis
favourite animal	cat / dog	cat / dog
thinks the worst thing about England is	the weather / crime	the weather / crime

3 Listen again and find words or expressions to show the following:

a) Asking someone's opinion ....

b) Agreeing with someone's positive opinion ....

c) Showing surprise ....

d) Changing the subject ....

e) Asking someone to agree with you ....

f) Agreeing with someone's negative opinion ....

4 What's a typical person from your country like? Are you typical? Discuss in pairs, using the above words and expressions.

26 Fox-hunting

1 Describe what is happening in these pictures. How do you feel about them?

2 Listen to Wendy and Stephen talking about fox-hunting. Look at the sentences below. Match the opinions to the right person. Write S for Stephen's opinion or W for Wendy's opinion.

a) It's wrong to kill foxes for fun. ☐

b) Foxes eat chickens and other farm animals. ☐

c) Animals don't suffer much when people kill them for meat. ☐

d) Dogs get hurt in fox-hunts. ☐

e) It's dangerous to kill foxes with poison. ☐

f) It's natural for dogs to kill foxes. ☐

3 Complete the table, then listen again to check your answers.

Noun	Adjective
cruelty	
beauty	
pain	
	poisonous
danger	
	diseased

4 Discussion. Tick (✓) the sentences you agree with.

Fox-hunting isn't cruel because ...

foxes are pests. They eat chickens from farms. ☐

there are too many foxes in the countryside. ☐

foxes die quickly in fox-hunts. It can take hours for foxes to die in traps. ☐

foxes can escape. ☐

Fox-hunting is cruel because ...

the foxes have a painful death. ☐

the foxes often fight the dogs before they die, so it's painful for dogs, too. ☐

foxes are useful because they kill animals that eat crops like rabbits. ☐

it is difficult for foxes to escape because dogs can run further than they can. ☐

Discuss your ideas in groups. Then take a vote on the following:

Fox-hunting should be banned. Do you agree or not?

27 Your favourite sport

1 Which sports do you need this equipment for? Write the sports next to the correct verbs.

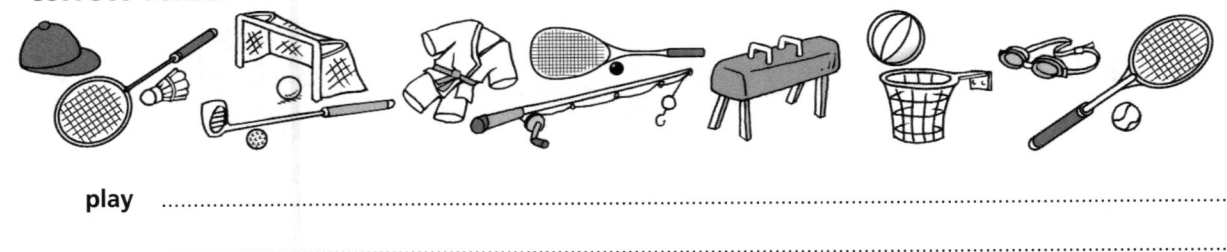

play ....

do ....

go ....

2 Listen to Kate, Simon, Jennifer and Adam describing their favourite sports and complete the sentences below. Then listen to the recording again and write down each person's favourite sport.

Kate

a) There are .... players in a team.

b) Shaquille O'Neal is .... metres, ... centimetres tall.

Kate's favourite sport is ....

Simon

c) There are four quarters. Each quarter is .... minutes long.

d) The playing field is 110 metres long and .... metres wide.

Simon's favourite sport is ....

Jennifer

e) People play this game in more than .... different countries.

f) The ball is only .... centimetres wide.

Jennifer's favourite sport is ....

Adam

g) There is a big championship every .... years.

h) It comes from a Chinese game, which is .... years old.

Adam's favourite sport is ....

3 Work in groups. Think of a new game and write some rules for it. Explain it to another group – would they like to play it?

4 The information below shows what four British sportsmen earned in 2003.

Lennox Lewis (now retired boxer)	£16 million
David Beckham (footballer)	£6.5 million
David Coulthard (racing driver)	£5 million
Darren Clarke (golfer)	£4 million

Do you think they deserve these salaries? Read the views of some different people. Which do you agree with? Discuss your views in a group.

a) *It really depends upon the sport involved. A Formula 1 racing driver deserves more than a footballer because motor racing is more dangerous.*

b) *I think sportspeople at their peak deserve what they earn. Sportspeople give lot of entertainment to people of this troubled world.*

c) *When I read of top sportsmen earning millions of pounds, and then read about the salaries of our brave firemen who often save lives even though they themselves might die, I think something is wrong.*

28 The Band

1) Discuss these questions in groups.

1 Have you ever
   a) given money to charity? ☐
   b) volunteered to help a charity? ☐
   c) tried to raise money for a charity? ☐

2 What kind of charity would you like to help?
   a) a children's charity ☐
   b) an animal charity ☐
   c) a medical charity, e.g. cancer ☐

3 Which of these sponsored events would you like to do?
   a) a 20 kilometre walk ☐
   b) a 24 hour dance (a group of you take turns to dance for 24 hours) ☐
   c) an eat-in (how much ice cream can you eat in 1 hour) ☐

2) Natasha, Jane, Dave and Andy are good friends. They have a plan for raising money. Listen to Part 1 and answer the questions.

a) What kind of charity are they raising money for? ....
b) Why are they forming a band? ....
c) Who can play the guitar? ....
d) Does Natasha or Andy want to sing? ....
e) What is Jane going to do? ....
f) Which song are they going to sing? ....
g) What is the problem? ....

3) Look at this dilemma.

What must Andy, Dave and Jane do? Give your opinion.

a) Tell Natasha that her singing is terrible and she must leave the band. ☐
b) Let her stay in the band so she doesn't get upset. ☐
c) Persuade her to do something else for the charity. ☐

4) Listen to Part 2 and answer the questions. Then look at the dilemma.

a) What did Andy, Dave and Jane decide to do? ....
b) Did they make much money? ....
c) Who are 'Gameboy'? ....
d) Was the concert a success? ....
e) Who speaks to Dave after the concert and why? ....

Look at this dilemma.

What must Dave do? Give your opinion.

a) Join 'Gameboy'. ☐   b) Stay with Andy. ☐
c) Join 'Gameboy' but not tell Andy and continue to play with him. ☐

5) Listen to find out what Dave does.

29 The End of Term

1 What will you do during your summer holiday? Tick (✔) the boxes.

	Yes	No
I'll lie in.	☐	☐
I'll watch a lot of TV.	☐	☐
I'll go shopping with my friends.	☐	☐
I'll do some studying.	☐	☐
I'll eat lots of ice cream.	☐	☐
I'll help my parents.	☐	☐
I'll go to a theme park.	☐	☐
I'll sunbathe on the beach.	☐	☐
I'll play lots of sports.	☐	☐
I'll get a job.	☐	☐

2 Jane, Natasha, Dave and Andy are at the same school. It is near the end of term and they are getting ready for sports day. Listen to Part 1. Which of these sentences does Jane say?

a) I was in the team last year. ☐

b) Great, I'm in the team. ☐

c) Nor am I. ☐

d) It's a shame that you aren't in the team with me. ☐

e) I'm so disappointed. ☐

f) We're going to the cinema tonight. ☐

g) I'd love to, but I can't. ☐

h) I don't want to be in the team. ☐

Look at the things Jane says. Why does she say them?

3 Jane is not happy. She says 'I don't want to be in the team.' Look at her choices. What would you do?

a) Ask the teacher to let her leave the team. ☐

b) Take part in the race. ☐

c) Tell the teacher she has hurt her leg and can't run. ☐

TIMESAVER ELEMENTARY LISTENING discussion – dilemmas 2

4 🎧 **Listen to Part 2. Tick the correct boxes, YES or NO.**

		YES	NO
a)	Jane takes part in the sports day.	☐	☐
b)	Her friends are not interested in what Jane is doing.	☐	☐
c)	Jane does the long jump.	☐	☐
d)	Jane is winning but then she is beaten.	☐	☐
e)	The holidays are in six weeks' time.	☐	☐
f)	Dave likes Jane.	☐	☐
g)	The girls decide to go to the cinema to see a Leonardo DiCaprio film.	☐	☐
h)	Andy asks Jane out.	☐	☐

5 **Now Jane has another dilemma. What would you do if you were her?**

a) Tell Andy she can't go to the cinema with him. ☐
b) Tell Natasha she's going to go out with Andy instead. ☐
c) Invite Natasha and Dave to the cinema as well. ☐

6 🎧 **Listen to Part 3 and answer the questions.**

a) What does Jane decide to do?
....

b) Did you agree with her choice?
....

c) Do you think Natasha is a good friend? Why?
....

d) Do the girls watch their film?
....

e) Is everyone happy? Why?
....

7 🎧 **Listen to the song and fill the gaps with the correct verbs.**

> relax   singing   eat   walking   have   swimming   leave   play   drink   go   get   watch

─────────────── **SUMMER'S COMING** ───────────────

It won't be long till summer's here.
The most fantastic time of year.
No more books and no more school.
We'll be (1)........................... in the pool.
It's gonna be hot even in the shade
So we'll (2)............... ice cream and (3)............... lemonade.

Chorus
Summer's coming, summer's coming.
Birds are (4)..........................., and the bees are humming.
The sun is out. The sky is clear
'Cos summer's nearly here.

We'll (5)........................... a picnic by the lake
Chocolate, strawberries, crisps and cake
And when we've eaten all we can

We'll just (6)........................... and get a tan.
We'll go (7)........................... in the park
And (8)........................... a movie when it's dark.

(Chorus)

We'll go down to the seaside,
Go to the funfair, (9)........................... on a ride
We'll (10)........................... all our problems far behind
'Cos summer's here at last.

At weekends, we'll (11)........................... to the coast
That's the place that we like the most.
We can (12)........................... tennis on the sand,
Or walk together hand in hand.
And when the setting sun goes down,
We'll take a walk into the town.

(Chorus)

30 Oliver Twist

1 Look at the picture. This is something you will hear about in the story of *Oliver Twist* by Charles Dickens. Do this puzzle and find out what it is.

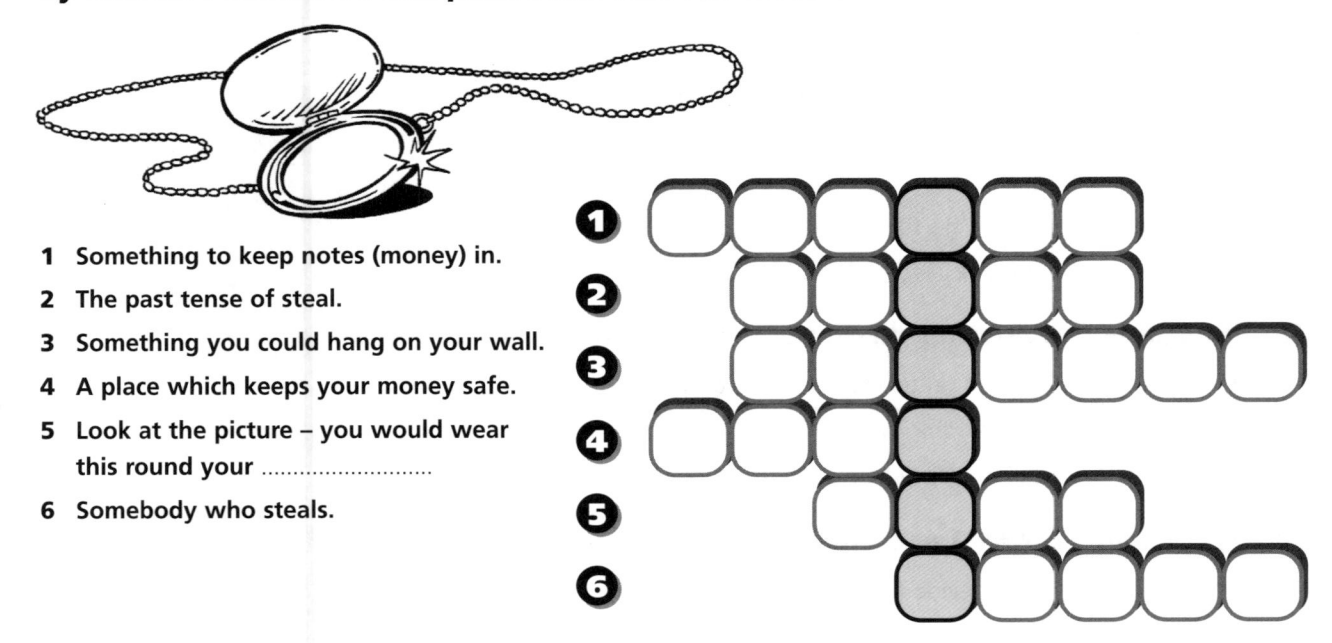

1 Something to keep notes (money) in.
2 The past tense of steal.
3 Something you could hang on your wall.
4 A place which keeps your money safe.
5 Look at the picture – you would wear this round your ....
6 Somebody who steals.

2 Here are some other words you will come across in the story. Choose five or six of them and make your own puzzle up. The mystery word can be your surprise!

> punishment   nurse   library   horrible   gold   money   kidnap   arrest

3 Look at these characters from the story. Think of two adjectives to describe each one.

Oliver   The Artful Dodger   Fagin   Mr Brownlow

Now listen. Do you think you were right? Can you add any more adjectives?

TIMESAVER ELEMENTARY LISTENING literature

4 Read the sentences about the story. Put the correct verbs in the gaps and then listen to the tape to check your answers.

> tried   visited   walked   promised   lived   pushed   asked   looked after   wanted   decided   showed   stayed

Oliver (1) *lived* in a workhouse. He didn't have enough food and he (2)............................ for more.

He (3)............................ to leave the workhouse.

He (4)............................ to London.

He (5)............................ with Fagin and the Artful Dodger.

The Artful Dodger (6)............................ to steal Mr Brownlow's wallet.

Mr Brownlow (7)............................ Oliver.

Fagin and the Artful Dodger (8)............................ a big house and (9)............................ Oliver through a window.

Mr Brownlow (10)............................ Oliver a gold locket.

Mr Brownlow (11)............................ to help Oliver's mother a long time ago. Now Mr Brownlow (12)............................ to help Oliver.

5 Listen to the verbs from the story. Do they end with a 'd' sound, a 't' sound or an 'id' sound? Put the verbs into the correct column.

'd' sound	't' sound	'id' sound
tried	walked	visited

6 Match the sentence halves about the story.

1 Oliver was a poor boy
2 The Artful Dodger was a thief
3 Fagin and the Artful Dodger took Oliver to a house
4 Mr Brownlow showed Oliver a locket
5 Oliver looked like the lady in the picture

a) that took Mr Brownlow's wallet.
b) that belonged to Oliver's mother.
c) that was in Mr Brownlow's house.
d) that lived in a London workhouse.
e) that they wanted to rob.

Now write out the sentences replacing *that* with *who* or *which*.

7 Tick the boxes.

I enjoyed the story. ☐   I would like to read the whole story. ☐
I didn't enjoy the story. ☐   I wouldn't like to read the whole story. ☐

Write two sentences explaining your choices.

....

....

31 A Christmas Carol

1 When do people in your country have days off work? Tick the holidays you have.

Christmas ☐	Easter ☐	Other ....
New Year ☐	May Day ☐	....
Eid el Fitr ☐	Children's Day ☐	....
Independence Day ☐	Divali ☐	....

What do people do on these days?

2 You are going to hear a Christmas story called *A Christmas Carol* by Charles Dickens. The main characters are Bob Cratchit, his wife, Bob's employer, whose name is Scrooge, and … some ghosts.

Bob Cratchit   Mrs Cratchit   Scrooge

Read through the sentences then listen and tick Yes or No.

	Yes	No
a) Scrooge was a kind employee.	☐	☐
b) Scrooge was happy to give Bob a holiday on Christmas Day.	☐	☐
c) Tiny Tim is ill.	☐	☐
d) Jacob Marley was Bob's work colleague.	☐	☐
e) Scrooge used to be married.	☐	☐
f) The Cratchits have more than one child.	☐	☐
g) The second ghost showed the Cratchits having a huge Christmas lunch.	☐	☐
h) The last ghost took Scrooge to a cemetery.	☐	☐
i) Scrooge died.	☐	☐
j) Scrooge became a better employer.	☐	☐

TIMESAVER ELEMENTARY LISTENING literature

3) Complete the sentences from the story by writing words for the pictures. Then listen again to check.

The ghost showed Scrooge things from his past. There was a (1)  ....

A beautiful girl was (2)  .... She was Scrooge's fiancée, but she married someone else because Scrooge was mean to her. Scrooge was very (3)  ....

Next, the (4)  .... of Christmas present visited Scrooge. He showed him Bob Cratchit's (5)  .... The family were having Christmas dinner.

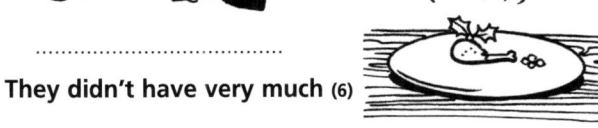

They didn't have very much (6) .... , but they were very (7)  ....

Scrooge looked at Tiny Tim. He was very (8)  .... Scrooge was worried about him.

4) Tick the boxes.

I enjoyed the story. ☐   I would like to read the whole story. ☐
I didn't enjoy the story. ☐   I wouldn't like to read the whole story. ☐

Write two sentences explaining your choices.

....

....

32 Robin Hood

1 Look at the characters in the story. What do you know about the Robin Hood legend? Match the descriptions to each person.

Robin Hood The Sheriff of Nottingham  John Little  Friar Tuck

a) He was a tall man. ....

b) He was quite fat. ....

c) He was very mean. ....

d) The Sheriff of Nottingham hated him. ....

e) He was cruel. ....

f) He was religious. ....

g) He was a good friend to Robin. ....

h) He could shoot well with a bow and arrow. ....

2 Listen to the story of Robin Hood and choose the correct answer, A, B or C. In this story Robin meets a knight.

1 Robin Hood was in prison because

　A he shot some deer in the forest. ☐

　B he killed the Sheriff of Nottingham. ☐

　C he was hungry. ☐

2 Friar Tuck came to see Robin Hood because

　A the Sheriff wanted him to. ☐

　B the King wanted him to. ☐

　C he wanted to give him some food. ☐

3 Robin was .... than John Little.

　A bigger and stronger

　B smaller

　C bigger and fatter

4 When Robin speaks to the knight, he is

　A by himself. ☐

　B with a group of men. ☐

　C with John Little and Friar Tuck. ☐

5 The knight is unhappy because

　　A he owes the Sheriff a lot of money. ☐

　　B the Sheriff borrowed money from him. ☐

　　C he is going to get a new castle. ☐

6 Robin and his men steal from

　　A wealthy people. ☐

　　B poor people. ☐

　　C beautiful people. ☐

7 The knight is

　　A sad his daughter married Robin Hood. ☐

　　B upset his daughter is leaving his castle. ☐

　　C is pleased his daughter married the Sheriff. ☐

8 The Sheriff of Nottingham

　　A gave up fighting Robin Hood. ☐

　　B carried on fighting Robin Hood. ☐

　　C thought he could beat Robin Hood. ☐

3 🎧 2/20 **Listen again. What do you find out about Maid Marian? Write three sentences.**

....

....

....

4 **Put the verbs in brackets into the past simple.**

　　a) Robin's parents .... (die) when he was young.

　　b) Robin .... (grow up) in Sherwood Forest.

　　c) The sheriff .... (put) Robin in prison for killing deer.

　　d) Robin .... (win) a fight against John Little.

　　e) Robin and John Little .... (become) good friends.

　　f) Robin and his men .... (steal) money from the rich to help the poor knight.

　　g) Robin often .... (give) money to the poor.

　　h) Robin and Marian .... (get) married.

　　i) The Sheriff of Nottingham .... (catch) John Little and wanted to kill him.

　　j) The Sheriff of Nottingham .... (fight) Robin but he didn't win.

5 **The story of Robin Hood is a "legend". In other words, it might not be true but it is very famous. Do you know any legends from your own country? Work in pairs to tell the story.**

OR

Use the internet to find out about one of these legends. Write the story to show to another pair. You will have to use the simple past tense.

Jason and the Golden Fleece

King Arthur and the Knights of the Round Table

33 The Hound of the Baskervilles

1 Here are some words you will hear in *The Hound of the Baskervilles* by Arthur Conan Doyle. Match them with the pictures.

1 hound ☐
2 devil ☐
3 scared ☐
4 footprint ☐
5 moor ☐
6 swamp ☐

a ☐
b ☐
c ☐
d ☐
e ☐
f ☐

2 Listen. How many people die in this story?

3 Listen again and read the sentences. Then tick Yes or No.

		YES	NO
a)	Hugo Baskerville was killed by the devil's hound.	☐	☐
b)	Sir Henry believes the story about the hounds.	☐	☐
c)	Sir Charles was related to Sir Henry.	☐	☐
d)	Sir Charles was bitten by a hound.	☐	☐
e)	Sherlock Holmes goes to Baskerville Hall with Sir Henry.	☐	☐
f)	Stapleton's house is next to Baskerville Hall.	☐	☐
g)	It's dangerous to walk on the moors because of the hounds.	☐	☐
h)	Sherlock Holmes suspects Stapleton of killing Sir Charles.	☐	☐
i)	A hound chases Sir Henry.	☐	☐
j)	Watson kills the hound.	☐	☐
k)	The hound belonged to Mrs Stapleton.	☐	☐
l)	Stapleton dies in a swamp.	☐	☐
m)	Everyone knew that Stapleton and Sir Henry were relatives.	☐	☐
n)	Stapleton wanted to own Baskerville Hall.	☐	☐

4 🎧 **Listen to the introduction to the story again. Read the following passage and correct the mistakes.**

A few years ago there was a kind man called Charles Baskerville. He was in love with a lady who loved him.

One morning, he locked her in a cellar at Baskerville Hall. She climbed out of a window and ran away. Hugo rode after her with his horses. He asked the police to help him find the girl and the devil's hound ran after her. When the police found Hugo the next afternoon, he was dead. The devil's hound was biting his leg.

5 **Now ask and answer questions about the passage in exercise 4.**

a) when / Hugo Baskerville / live *When did Hugo Baskerville live? He lived many years ago.*

b) what / Hugo Baskerville / like? ....

c) who / he / love? ....

d) where / Hugo / lock / the girl? ....

e) what / she / do? ....

f) who / chase / her? ....

g) who / Hugo / ask / for help? ....

h) what / chase / Hugo? ....

i) when / they / find / Hugo? ....

j) what / happen / him? ....

6 🎧 **Now listen to two people talking about this story. What adjectives do they use to describe Sherlock Holmes, Stapleton and the hound? Listen and write two adjectives in each box.**

Sherlock Holmes is	Stapleton is	The hound is

7 **What do you know about Sherlock Holmes? Look at the pictures and write some sentences about him. Use the internet to help you (eg www.sherlock-holmes.co.uk) and add any other information you find out.**

221b Baker Street

34 Romeo and Juliet

1 Romeo and Juliet by William Shakespeare is a story of love and hate. Look at the words in the box and write them in the correct column.

> detest   adore   to be fond of   can't stand   loathe   to be crazy about   to be keen on   can't bear

Love	Hate

2 Look at the pictures of these characters. Then read the following statements about the story and answer the questions before you listen.

a) Juliet's mother sees Romeo dancing with her daughter. Is she happy? ....

b) Juliet's parents find a suitable man for her to marry. Is Juliet happy? ....

c) Juliet goes to speak to the Friar. Can he help her? ....

d) Romeo's friend gives him some news. Is Romeo happy? ....

Romeo Montague

Juliet Capulet

The Friar, an important religious man

Lady Capulet

TIMESAVER ELEMENTARY LISTENING literature

3 🎧 **Listen again and put the pictures in the correct order.**

a) ☐   b) ☐   c) ☐

d) ☐   e) ☐   f) ☐

4 **William Shakespeare was English but *Romeo and Juliet* takes place in a different country. Read the sentences below and choose the correct letters to find the name of the country.**

   a) Romeo asked Juliet to dance so Ⓢ / because Ⓘ he thought she was beautiful.
   b) Lady Capulet didn't want Juliet to speak to Romeo so Ⓟ / because Ⓣ he was a Montague.
   c) Romeo waited outside Juliet's bedroom so Ⓐ / because Ⓔ he could talk to her.
   d) Juliet didn't want to marry Paris so Ⓘ / because Ⓛ she was married to Romeo.
   e) Romeo was in town so Y / because Ⓝ he didn't get the Friar's letter.

Romeo and Juliet lived in __ __ __ __ __ .
                           a b c d e

5 **Now retell the story in your own words. Use the pictures in Exercise 3 and the sentences in Exercise 4 to help you.**

35 Othello

1 You are going to hear the story of Othello by William Shakespeare. Here are the main characters.

Othello, leader of the army of Venice

Cassio, Othello's lieutenant

Iago, a man in Othello's army

Desdemona, Othello's wife

Emilia, Desdemona's maid and Iago's wife

In this story, some people are very jealous. Look at these pictures. What do you think the connection is?

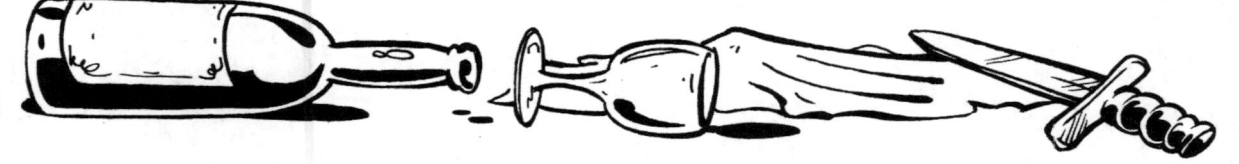

2 Listen to the play and try to explain why the above pictures are important.

a) wine ....

b) handkerchief ....

c) dagger ....

3 Listen again. Read the play and complete the gaps.

Presenter Othello is a lucky man. He has an important job and a beautiful wife. Almost everyone likes him. But Othello has got one enemy – Iago. Iago is an evil man. He works for Othello. He wanted to be his lieutenant, but Othello (1)........................ Cassio. Now Iago (2)........................ Othello. Iago wants revenge against Othello and Cassio.

One night, Iago goes for a walk and meets Cassio.

Iago (*Thinking*) There's Cassio. He's a good soldier, but he likes alcohol (3)........................ much. I've got a good idea.

Iago Cassio, you work too hard! You must relax. How (4)........................ a glass of wine?

Cassio All right, but only one. I (5)........................ get up early tomorrow.

Presenter *Three hours later*

Man Ha, ha. Your nose is red. It looks (6)........................ a strawberry.

Cassio	Idiot! No one jokes about me.
Othello	Who is making all this noise? Cassio – you're drunk! I can't have a lieutenant who gets drunk and has fights. You (7)............................ leave your job.
Presenter	Next day…
Cassio	Why was I (8)............................ stupid? I loved my job.
Iago	Don't worry. Go and see Othello's wife and tell her you are (9)............................ . Desdemona can ask Othello to make you his lieutenant again. He does anything for his wife.
Presenter	Cassio visits Desdemona. She (10)............................ to help. But as he leaves the house …
Iago	Who is that man leaving your house?
Othello	He looks like Cassio.
Iago	That's strange! Why is Cassio (11)............................ your wife in secret?
Desdemona	Othello, I was thinking about poor Cassio. He was a good lieutenant. Why (12)............................ give him another chance?
Othello	Let me think about it. (*Thinking*) Why is she thinking (13)............................ Cassio? Is she in love with him? Of course not! She loves me.
Emilia	Look, Desdemona dropped her favourite handkerchief. It's the one Othello gave her when they (14)............................ - Desdemona!
Iago	Don't call her. They are busy. Give the handkerchief to me. I can return it (15)............................ .
Iago	(*Thinking*) I'm going to put this in Cassio's room.
Presenter	Next day…
Cassio	(*Thinking*) Where did this handkerchief come from?
Iago	What has Cassio got? Is that Desdemona's handkerchief?
Othello	(*Thinking*) Oh no, it's true! Desdemona loves Cassio. She looks sweet and (16)............................ , but she is a liar.
Presenter	That night.
Desdemona	Othello, is that you?
Othello	Yes, but perhaps you wanted someone (17)............................ .
Desdemona	What do you (18)............................ ?
Othello	I saw Cassio with the handkerchief that I gave you. I loved you, (19)............................ you lied to me. Now you must die.
Presenter	Emilia comes (20)............................ the room.
Emilia	I heard noises. What's (21)............................ ? Desdemona!
Othello	I loved her, but she loved Cassio. I killed her.
Emilia	Help! Help! Othello killed his wife.
Man	What (22)............................ ?
Othello	She loved Cassio. She gave him her handkerchief. I saw him with it.
Emilia	No, she (23)............................ the handkerchief. My husband took it.
Iago	Shut up, Emilia!
Emilia	I'm dying!
Man	Take Iago, men.
Othello	Yes, take him, but don't kill him. I (24)............................ him to live and suffer. But Desdemona is dead so I must die, (25)............................ .

4 **Look at these letters to a problem page. Can you match each letter to a character from the play? Then write a letter giving advice to one of these characters.**

Cassio ☐   Othello ☐   Iago ☐

A I hate my boss. He didn't give me the job that I want. Now I can't stop thinking about how much I hate him. What must I do?

B I am an idiot. I got drunk and I had a fight with another man. My boss saw me and I lost my job. What can I do?

C I love my wife so much. But now I know that she is a liar and she loves another man. What must I do?

TIMESAVER ELEMENTARY LISTENING literature

36 Treasure Island

1 Answer the questions and find out where the treasure is buried.

a) It's not under the tallest thing on the island.
b) You don't need to get your feet wet to find it.
c) You won't see any dangerous animals near it.
d) There's a lot of grass growing around it.
e) Butterflies are very fond of the area.
f) It's near the coast.

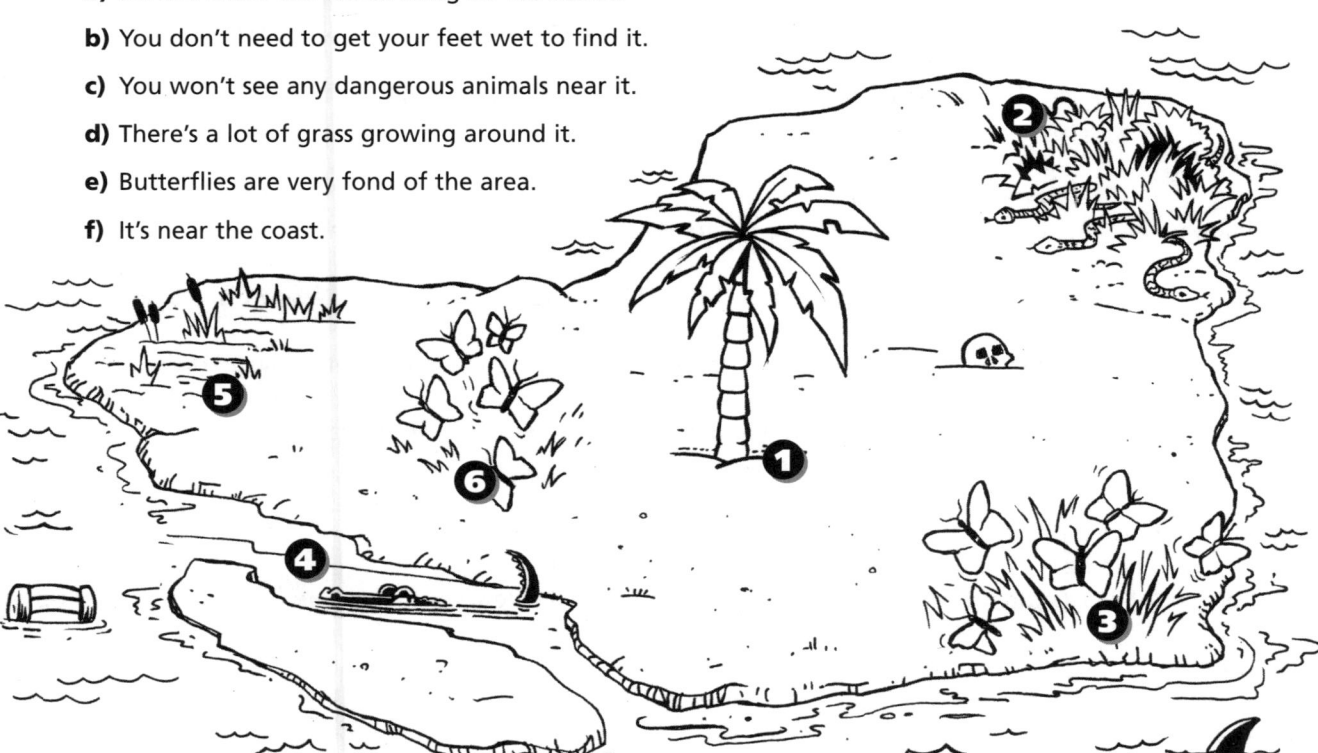

2 Here are the characters you will hear in Treasure Island by Robert Louis Stevenson.

Jim Hawkins – a young boy

Dr Livesey – a doctor and Jim's friend

Captain Smollet – an honest captain

Long John Silver – an evil pirate

Ben Gunn – a shipwrecked sailor

If you were acting in the film of this book, which character would you like to play?

literature

3 🎧 Listen to the story and choose the correct answer, A, B or C.

1 How did Jim get the Treasure Map?
  A A dying man gave it to him. ☐
  B He stole it from a dying man. ☐
  C Dr Livesey gave it to him. ☐

2 What is Dr Livesey worried about?
  A Jim is too young to go to sea. ☐
  B There are a lot of pirates about. ☐
  C He was a sailor a long time ago but now he isn't very careful. ☐

3 What does Long John Silver say his job is?
  A a sailor ☐
  B an adventurer ☐
  C a cook ☐

4 Who doesn't Captain Smollet trust?
  A Long John Silver ☐
  B all the men on the ship ☐
  C Dr Livesey ☐

5 What is Long John Silver going to do first when they get to the island?
  A kill Jim and his friends ☐
  B steal the treasure ☐
  C look for the treasure ☐

6 Who do Jim and his friends meet when they arrive on the island?
  A another pirate ☐
  B the owner ☐
  C a helpful man ☐

7 What did Long John Silver do with the captain and the doctor?
  A They fought with them. ☐
  B They killed them. ☐
  C They took them prisoner. ☐

8 What did the pirates find?
  A the treasure ☐
  B a hole ☐
  C nothing ☐

9 Why did the pirates fight?
  A Because they had drunk too much. ☐
  B Because they couldn't find the treasure. ☐
  C Because they didn't want to share the treasure. ☐

10 Where was the treasure at the end of the story?
  A in a cave ☐
  B in the sea ☐
  C on Jim's ship ☐

4 Now you have listened to the story, look at the question in exercise 2 again. Do you still want to be the same character? Why? / Why not?

5 🎧 Listen to the list of words. Tick (✔) the words that rhyme with the first word in each list. Put a cross (✗) next to the words that don't rhyme.

1	treasure	measure ☐	either ☐
2	know	how ☐	so ☐
3	fight	night ☐	bite ☐
4	young	long ☐	sung ☐
5	boat	note ☐	coat ☐
6	steal	meal ☐	sail ☐
7	really	early ☐	nearly ☐
8	choose	lose ☐	loose ☐

Recording Script

Introduction

The recording script can be photocopied for students. After they have listened, they can underline sections where they have found the answers and confirm they are correct. It can be used to extend vocabulary and also to practise intonation by asking students to read the short dialogues aloud.

1 A Surprise Lunch

Exercise 3, Part 1
Presenter: It's lunchtime. Max is opening his packed lunch.
Max: Oh no! Cheese sandwiches and an apple again. I always have cheese sandwiches and an apple. Boring!
Robbie: I've got peanut butter sandwiches, a banana, a yoghurt and a chocolate chip muffin!
Presenter: The next day
Max: Oh no. Not again.
Robbie: Have you got boring cheese sandwiches and an apple?
Max: Yes. What have you got?
Robbie: I've got a roll, crisps, fruit salad and a doughnut.
Presenter: Next week
Robbie: I know, I know. You've got cheese sandwiches again.
Max: I don't want to see another cheese sandwich in my life!
Presenter: At home
Max: Mum, have we got anything different for my sandwiches? I like ham, eggs, jam, and chocolate spread.
Mum: OK, no problem.
Brother: (thinks) Max always wants something different. I've got an idea.
Presenter: The next day
Brother: Heh heh!
Presenter: At school
Robbie: Cheese sandwiches again Max?
Max: No. I'm sure I've got something different today.

Exercise 4, Part 2
Presenter: Max opens his lunch box
Robbie: What have you got?
Max: What's this? Spider and chocolate spread sandwiches! Yuk!
Brother: Heh heh! Happy Halloween Max!

Exercise 5
Presenter: Max
Max: I've got an apple, a chocolate bar, a bottle of water and a cheese sandwich.
Presenter: Jennie
Jennie: I've got a banana, some crisps, some Coke, and a salad sandwich.
Presenter: Robbie
Robbie: I've got an apple, a yoghurt, a cake and a sandwich.

2 Christmas is Coming

Exercise 2, Part 1
Presenter: It's four days before Christmas
Will: It's nearly Christmas. I'm so excited. I wonder what I've got.
Vicki: I know what I've got. DVDs and a mini-disc player. They're in my parents' wardrobe.
Will: Cool! I wonder where my present is. Come on!
Presenter: Will and Vicki check the bedroom
Vicki: Is it in the wardrobe?
Will: No, nothing. Only clothes.
Vicki: Maybe it's under the bed?
Will: No, nothing here. Only smelly socks!
Will: Look under the stairs. Be careful!
Vicki: Yuk, Will. There are spiders in here.
Presenter: Now they check the lounge
Vicki: Look behind the sofa!
Will: Aha! Here's a present. I'm sure it's mine.
Vicki: Quick, open it before your parents come home.
Will: Yuk! It's an orange shirt! How disgusting!

Exercise 3, Part 2
Dad: Will! What are you doing?
Will: Er, looking at this, er, beautiful shirt!
Dad: That's good. You can have it for Christmas and Uncle Les can have your present.
Presenter: Christmas Day
Uncle Les: Happy Christmas Will. Nice shirt! I love my new Playstation, what a fantastic present!
Will: Doh!

Exercise 4
Dad: I'm in my bedroom with the presents.
I've got two CDs and a Playstation game for Will. I'm putting them on the wardrobe.
I've got some perfume for Will's mum. It smells strange! I'm putting it in the drawers.
I've got some chocolates for Will's grandma. I'm putting them behind the wardrobe.
I've some new socks for grandpa. They are horrible, but he likes them. I'm putting them under the bed.

3 The Babysitter

Exercise 2
Max: Mum, have you got £30? I'm bored of my PlayStation games.
Mum: No Max! You already have your pocket money this week!
Jennie: If you need money, call Mrs Wilson. She needs a babysitter on Saturday.
Max: Babysitting? Me? Oh OK!
Presenter: It's seven o'clock on Saturday. At Mrs Wilson's house.
Mrs Wilson: Hi Max! Alex is sleeping. If you're hungry, take what you want from the fridge. Here's my mobile phone number. I'm back at half past nine.
Max: No problem!
Max: This is easy.
Presenter: Ten minutes later
Kid: I'm thirsty. I need a drink.
Max: OK. Here's some orange juice. Now back to bed.
Presenter: Five minutes later
Kid: Max, I'm hungry now. I'd like something to eat.
Max: Here's an apple.
Kid: No, I'd like a chocolate bar.
Max: Oh, OK. Go to bed.
Presenter: Two minutes later
Kid: I'm bored! I'd like to play a game.
Max: OK. But then it's bedtime for you.
Presenter: An hour later
Max: Bedtime!

Kid: I always have a story before bed. Read me a story, please Max.
Max: Oh, OK.
Kid: Here you are.
Max: Clifford and Bob are going to ... then ... er ... zzzzzzz!
Presenter: Max is asleep
Presenter: At half past nine
Mrs Wilson: Max!

Exercise 3
Presenter: one
Presenter: Grrr. I'm angry!
Presenter: two
Presenter: I'm sleepy.
Presenter: three
Presenter: I'm happy.
Presenter: four
Presenter: I'm hungry!

Exercise 4
Presenter: one
Max: When Mrs Wilson leaves at seven o'clock, Alex is sleeping.
Presenter: two
Max: At ten minutes past seven, she's thirsty. She wants something to drink.
Presenter: three
Max: At quarter past seven she is hungry. She wants a chocolate bar.
Presenter: four
Max: At twenty past seven she wants to play a game.
Presenter: five
Max: At twenty past eight she wants a story.
Presenter: six
Max: At half past eight I'm asleep!

4 The Maths Test
Exercises 2 and 3
Presenter: Will is getting ready for school.
Mum: Come on Will! It's ten to nine already.
Will: Oh no, it's Tuesday the sixth!
(thinks) We've got a big maths test at school today.
Mum: Are you all right, dear?
Will: Er, no. I don't feel well. I feel sick and hot.
Mum: Let me see.
Will: Ouch, it hurts!
Mum: Go and lie down, Will.
Mum: Don't worry Will. The doctor is coming immediately!
Will: Oh no!
Will: Oh no, Mum. I don't like the doctor.
Doctor: What's the matter, Will?
Will: I feel sick and I've got stomach ache.
Doctor: I see.
Doctor: Oh dear. This is serious. Maybe it's appendicitis.
Will: (thinks) Oh no. I don't want to go to hospital!
Doctor: Take this medicine five times a day and no sweets or chocolate.
Will: Thank you doctor. I feel better already.
Doctor: (thinks) What a recovery!
Mum: Good. You can rest today and go back to school tomorrow.
Will: All right mum. (thinks) There are no maths tests tomorrow!
Presenter: Lunchtime
Vicki: Hi Will. It's Vicki. What's wrong? Why aren't you at school?
Will: Er.. I've got stomach ache. But I feel better now.
Vicki: Really? Mr Stropson is ill today too. The maths test is tomorrow!
Will: Oh no!

5 Will's T-shirt
Exercise 2
Presenter: It's Saturday morning
Mum: Oh Will. You can't wear that old T-shirt anymore.
Will: Why not? It's my favourite!
Mum: It's dirty and it's got a hole in it. Why don't you go shopping with Vicki and buy something nice? Here's ten pounds.
Vicki: Come on, Will. Let's go.
Mum: And this horrible T-shirt can go to the charity shop.
Presenter: In the department store
Will: Mmn, this is nice. Calvin Klein.
Snooty Assistant: Can I help you?
Will: How much is it?
Snooty Assistant: £75.
Will: Oh, it's too expensive.
Vicki: Let's go to a sports shop.
Will: These T-shirts are cool!
Assistant: You can try them on in this changing room.
Will: Oh! It's too big.
Will: Oh! It's too small.
Vicki: What about this?
Will: Are you mad? That's disgusting! I can't buy any of these clothes. They're too expensive, too small, too big or too disgusting. I hate shopping. I'm going home.
Will: What's this? I can't believe my eyes. My T-shirt! In a charity shop! What cheek!
Will: How much is the beautiful T-shirt in the window?
Old shop assistant: What? That old T-shirt? You can have it for £5.
Will: I'll take it.
Mum: Hello Will...Well, what have you got?
Will: This stylish T-shirt and it only cost £5. What a bargain!
Mum: I can't win!

6 Vicki's Pet
Exercise 2
Vicki: We're going on holiday next week. I can't look after Charlie, my hamster. Can you look after him?
Will: Of course I can. I love animals!
Vicki: Here's his seed and bedding. Give him fresh water every day. He can't have any chocolate or any biscuits.
Will: No problem!
Presenter: The next day
Will: Hello Charlie. Do you like this seed? Here's some crisps. They taste better than seed.
Presenter: The next day
Will: I don't know how you can drink only water. Have some Coke, it tastes nicer than water.
Presenter: Next week
Will: Poor Charlie. I don't know how you can live in that cage. Here. You can run here.
Bob: Hey, I think it's time to put Charlie back in his cage. Vicki is coming in an hour.
Will: He's not here. I can't find him! Where is he? Charlie!
Presenter: Later
Bob: Oh no. It's Vicki. Don't tell her about Charlie. Show her a video and I can look for Charlie.
Will: Er, hi Vicki, nice holiday? Come and watch my new video.

Vicki: Er, how's Charlie?
Will: Charlie? Oh, he's fine. Sit down. Do you like the video Charlie's Angels?
Vicki: Ouch! What's that?
Will: What's the matter?
Vicki: It's Charlie! In the sofa! What's he doing here?
Will: Er, watching his favourite film!

7 Travelling by Train

Exercise 2, Part 1
Will: It's Saturday at last! Mum, can I go skateboarding with my friends?
Mum: No, you can't. You are always on that thing. Why don't you go and visit Aunty Pat and Uncle Tom? Here's some money for the train and some flowers for Aunty.
Will: It's so far! And so boring!
Mum: Really Will? Do you want your pocket money this week?
Presenter: Will sees some of his school friends.
Bob: Hi Will. Mmm. Nice flowers!
Will: (thinks) How embarrassing!
Presenter: At the train station
Will: Single to Forest Hill, please.
Sales assistant: £3.60, please. Hurry up, the train leaves in one minute.
Will: Phew!

Exercise 3, Part 2
Aunty Pat: Hello dear. How are you?
Will: OK.
Aunty Pat: What's the matter?
Will: I'd like to go skateboarding today but mum says I can't.
Aunty Pat: Why not? Of course you can. Uncle Tom loves skateboarding. How about skateboarding with him?
Will: Uncle Tom? But he's too old!
Uncle Tom: Who's too old? Come on. Let's go!
Will and friends: Wow! He's excellent!
Will: Can I have a go now, Uncle Tom?
Uncle Tom: Just one more flip!!

Exercise 4
Will: Hello. A ticket to Forest Hill, please.
Station Assistant: Single or return?
Will: Return please.
Station Assistant: Are you under 16?
Will: Yes, I'm 12.
Station Assistant: Then you can have a child's ticket.
Will: How much is it?
Station Assistant: One child return to Forest Hill. That's £3.20.
Will: Here's £5.
Station Assistant: Thank you. Here's the change and your ticket. Goodbye!

8 Lucky Socks

Exercise 2
Presenter: Will is late for school, again.
Vicki: Hurry up, Will. We're late!
Will: I can't find any socks! How about these? Ugh, holes! Here's a pair. Yuck. They are so uncool!
Teacher 1: It's five past nine. That's the third time you are late. Detention!
Presenter: In class, later
Teacher 1: What are they? You mustn't wear green socks, Smith. Detention! Take them off immediately!
Will: OK, Sir.
Presenter: Next lesson
Teacher 2: Where are your socks Will? You must wear socks to school. Detention after school!
Will: But Mr Herbert has got them!
Vicki: Girls don't wear socks. Why do boys have to? It's very hot.
Teacher 2: Don't be cheeky. You can have a detention too!
Presenter: After school
Teacher 1: Now write 'I must not wear green socks' 100 times!
Will: I'm going to be late for the football match.
Presenter 1: At the school football match
Will: Sorry I'm late. Three detentions!
Friend: We're going to lose. We've only got 10 players.
Opposite team: Ugh! Look at that boy's socks!
Goalkeeper: Ha ha ha!
Will's team: It's a goal!
We are the champions!
Will: And all because of my lucky socks!

Exercise 3
Will: Here are my school rules. First of all teachers mustn't give you homework. You must listen to your Walkman in lessons. Oh, and you mustn't wear school uniform. No way! Rule number four, you must bring sweets and chewing gum to lessons – that's very important. And you must be late for lessons – at least five minutes. These are good school rules!

9 Eating Out

Exercise 2
Victoria: For a starter, I'd like the green salad. Then I'd like the fish.
Waitress: Green salad and the fish. Would madam like a dessert?
Victoria: Oh, OK. I'd like the strawberry ice cream please.
David: Mmn. For a starter I'd like the melon.
Waitress: Melon. OK. Anything else?
David: I'd like a pizza, er but I'm not sure which one.
Victoria: How about four-cheese pizza? That's nice.
David: OK. The four-cheese pizza and for dessert I'd like an ice cream.
Waitress: What flavour?
David: I don't know.
Waitress: We've got strawberry, chocolate, vanilla, peach, lemon, and pistachio nut.
David: Erm, er, erm er. Straw, er no, yes, chocolate, chocolate please!

Exercise 3
1 I'd like fish.
2 I like chicken.
3 Do you like chocolate ice cream?
4 What would you like?

Exercise 5
The Bubblegum Rap
I like strawberry, cherry
Cola too
Can be pink and can be blue
I don't care
It's no trouble
I just wanna blow that bubble

Chew with me
Chew and tap
That's the name of the bubble gum rap.

I've got banana, blueberry
Lemon and lime
Chew together
They'll turn to slime
Oh I don't care
It's no trouble
I just wanna blow that bubble.

It's sticky, it's like glue
Open up and
Start to chew
I don't care
It's no trouble
I just wanna blow that bubble

Chew with me
Chew and tap
You can do the bubble gum rap

Yep, I really love
My bubble gum
Not in school or
In front of Mum
But I make certain
I am sure
I put it in the bin
And not on the floor!

10 Summer Holidays

Exercise 2
Presenter: It's the first day of the summer holidays.
Max: Hooray! It's the holidays. Let's go to Brighton!
Robbie: Fantastic idea!
Presenter: In Brighton
Max: I love Brighton pier!
Robbie: I'm going to go on the mouse rollercoaster! It's cool.
Max: But we can't. We're too short.
Max: The dodgems are cool. We must go on the dodgems!
Man: Excuse me boys, how old are you?
Robbie and Max: We're thirteen and twelve.
Man: Sorry. One of you must be sixteen.
Max: How about going on the log flume?
Robbie: I can't. If my clothes get wet my mum is going to be angry with me!
Max: OK. Let's go to the stalls. We can try and win something.
Presenter: At the football stall
Robbie: Look, you must try to score a goal to win.
Max: Easy!
Presenter: Max shoots…
Presenter: …and misses
Max: I don't believe it!
Max: We've only got £2 now. Most of the rides are too expensive. Let's go home.
Robbie: Look, this game is cheap.
Presenter: Max throws the dart
Presenter: Max hits the target. He's a winner!
Max: Wow! What prize am I going to win?
Man: This cuddly toy!
Max: Oh no! How embarrassing!
Robbie: Lovely toy, Max!

Exercise 3
Max: I love the holidays. I've got six weeks with no school!
Robbie: But what are you going to do?
Max: On Monday, I'm going to go swimming.
On Tuesday, I'm going to go to the beach.
On Wednesday, I'm going to go to the pier.
On Thursday, I'm going to go to a museum.
On Friday, I'm going to play football with my friends.
On Saturday, I'm going to go to the shops.
On Sunday, I'm going to visit my cousins. They live in London.
Robbie: That's cool. But what are you going to do for the other five weeks?
Max: Five weeks? Oops! I don't know!

Exercise 4
David: I'm going to the beach today.
I'm going to take my sunglasses. I love my sunglasses – they are very important! I'm going to take some sun oil. I don't want to be red!
I'm going to take a ball to play football.
I'm going to take flip-flops too. I don't want sand in my trainers!
And I'm going to take a CD player to listen to my favourite music, rap.

11 The Mystery Picture

Exercise 2
In the middle of the picture, there's a big house. The house has got four windows, one in each corner. There's a door between the two windows at the bottom of the house. The door has got a round handle on the left. At the top of the door, there's the number of the house. It's one hundred and twenty six. The roof of the house looks like a triangle. The moon is in the sky. It looks like the letter 'c'. There are also three stars in the sky. There is a cat next to the house, on the left. It's fat and it's sitting down. On the other side of the house, there are four flowers.

12 American Festivals

Exercises 2 and 3
Vicky: This is my favourite festival. Children love it. They dress up as monsters or ghosts, then they go to visit their neighbours. Their neighbours have to give them sweets or chocolates. If they don't, the children give them a nasty surprise. This game is called trick or treat. For this festival lots of people have pumpkins outside their houses or in their windows.
Jeanette: This is a very special day because it is the first day of the year. On this day, lots of people make promises to themselves, called resolutions. People usually try to give up their bad habits.
Alex: This is a day in November. It is a religious festival, so lots of families go to church. They want to say thank you for their food. People often celebrate by meeting up with their brothers or sisters they haven't seen for a long time. They usually have a big family meal. The traditional food to eat is turkey.
Adam: This is the day that Americans celebrate their freedom. It's a day for the whole family to be together. They often go for picnics or have barbecues during the day and see fireworks in the evening. This day makes all American people feel proud to be American.

13 England vs America

Exercise 2
Andy: Jane do you prefer America or England?
Jane: I like America, but I prefer England. I think America is too big.
Natasha: I don't. I think it's good that everything is big in

America. In England the cinemas and theme parks are too small. Disney World is much better than the theme parks in England. I think America is really cool.
Dave: So do I. I went to America last year and it was amazing. The people are friendlier than the people in England and the food is great. In some restaurants in America you can eat as much as you want.
Jane: Yes. American food is really nice. I love burgers and chips, but they are very bad for you. Have you ever been to America, Andy?
Andy: No, but I've watched lots of programmes about it on television. I think America is cool, but it's very dangerous. In America, people can have guns. I prefer England. It's safer.
Natasha: England is safe, but it's boring. America is exciting. Kids who live in America are really lucky because they can see new films before anyone else.

14 India

Exercises 2 and 3

Sally Ann: Tom, you've been to India. What's it like?
Tom: Well, it's a big country with different regions. The Himalaya region has got some of the highest mountains in the world …
Sally Ann: Like Mount Everest?
Tom: No, Mount Everest is in Nepal, but India has got Kanchenjunga, the third highest mountain in the world.
Sally Ann: What are the cities like?
Tom: Indian cities can be very busy. Mumbai is the biggest city. More than 12 million people live there.
Sally Ann: Wow. There are a lot of people in India, aren't there?
Tom: Yes. Over 900 million people live there. The only country with more people is China.
Sally Ann: What language do people speak?
Tom: There are over 1,600 languages in India. Hindi is the official language but lots of people also speak English.
Sally Ann: And what animals live in India?
Tom: There are lots of interesting animals - panthers, leopards and cheetahs …
Sally Ann: Are there any tigers?
Tom: Yes, but tigers almost became extinct in India. The government made strict laws to protect them. Now there are thousands more.
Sally Ann: That's good. What are the people like?
Tom: Most people are very poor. Some people don't even have clean water.
Sally Ann: That's terrible, but are things getting better for Indian people?
Tom: Yes. Things are slowly getting better. The main trade is farming, but India has other successful industries - like film-making. India makes more films than any other country.

15 What Shall We Do?

Exercises 2 and 3

Jennifer: Great, school's finished! What do you want to do tonight?
Adam: Why don't you come to my house? We can play that new computer game.
Jennifer: No. Computer games are really boring.
Adam: OK, let's go swimming.
Jennifer: I don't like swimming. The water is always too cold.
Adam: How about going skateboarding?
Jennifer: I'm not very good at skateboarding. It's too difficult to stay on the skateboard.
Adam: Shall we go to the cinema, then?
Jennifer: I'd like to, but I haven't got enough money.
Adam: Do you want to go to the Internet café?
Jennifer: We did that yesterday.
Adam: OK, let's watch television.
Jennifer: Good idea!

16 A Phone Call from Jamaica

Exercises 2 and 3

Kate: Hello, 772 6273
Jennifer: Hello Kate, it's Jennifer.
Kate: Jennifer! How is your holiday in Jamaica going? Are you enjoying yourself?
Jennifer: Yes. Everyone's having a great time. We're all enjoying ourselves very much.
Kate: I'm not surprised. What's the weather like there?
Jennifer: It's very hot. Actually, I think it's a bit too hot. Dad burnt himself while he was sunbathing yesterday.
Kate: Oh dear. Is he all right?
Jennifer: Yes, he's fine, now. But parents are so embarrassing! Mum bought herself a reggae CD and now Mum and Dad are trying to teach themselves a Jamaican dance.
Kate: Are they good at dancing?
Jennifer: No, they're terrible.
Mum: Jennifer!
Jennifer: Just a minute, Mum's calling me. I think I'll have to go.
Kate: Bye bye, Jennifer. I'll see you soon.
Jennifer: Yes, but unfortunately the next time we see each other, we'll be at school.
Kate: Well, you're lucky. All my friends are on holiday, but I'm at home by myself.
Jennifer: Cheer up, Kate. I'll bring back a present for you. Goodbye.

17 Valentine's Day

Exercises 2 and 3

Kate: I love Valentine's Day. Getting a card from someone who likes you always makes you happy doesn't it?
Simon: I don't think so. I think that it's silly. Everyone wastes their money on cards and then they don't write their names in them, so you don't know who your card is from.
Kate: Yes, but having a secret card is really exciting, isn't it?
Simon: No, it's stupid.
Kate: Oh, I see. You didn't get a Valentine's card from anyone, did you?
Simon: Yes I did.
Kate: Well, where is it?
Simon: It's in my bag, but you don't really want to see it, do you?
Kate: Of course I do! I know all the girls in your class. I can tell you who it's from.
Simon: OK, here it is.
Kate: (Reading) 'To my wonderful Simon, You're so handsome and so clever. I think I'm going to love you forever' - I know this writing. You wrote this card, didn't you?
Simon: No, I didn't.
Kate: I know that you're lying. Your face is red.
Simon: OK, you're right, but you're not going to tell anyone, are you?
Kate: Let me think… not if you help me with my homework and

lend me your stereo and buy me some chocolate and lend me some money …

Exercise 4
1. Getting a card from someone who likes you always makes you happy, doesn't it?
2. Having a secret card is really exciting, isn't it?
3. You didn't get a Valentine's card from anyone, did you?
4. It's in my bag, but you don't really want to see it, do you?
5. You wrote this card, didn't you?
6. You're not going to tell anyone, are you?

18 Guy Fawkes

Exercises 2 and 3
1. King James the First was very unfair to Catholic people. Guy Fawkes was a Catholic and he hated the king. He joined a group of men who wanted to kill him.
2. They filled a cellar under the Houses of Parliament with gunpowder. They planned to light the gunpowder on November 5th when the king visited the Houses of Parliament.
3. But one of the men had a relative who often visited the Houses of Parliament. He warned his relative about the plan and his relative warned King James.
4. When Guy Fawkes entered the cellar on the night of November 5th, the king's men were already there.
5. They wanted to know the names of the other men in Guy Fawkes's group, so they tortured him until he confessed their names. They arrested the men and killed them. Guy Fawkes died with them.

19 Holiday Plans

Exercises 2 and 3
Paul: Where are you going for your summer holiday, Sally Ann?
Sally Ann: If I can save enough money, I'll go to America. I'd love to go to New Orleans. My best friend went there last year and she said it was fantastic. What about you?
Paul: My brother moved to Australia last year so if he invites me, I'll go there. I want to see the outback, enjoy the sun - and go surfing, of course.
Sally Ann: Mmm, that would be lovely, but what if he doesn't invite you?
Paul: I've always wanted to go to India, but I'll only go if I can take a month off work. India's such a fascinating place. You need to stay there for more than a week or two.
Sally Ann: That sounds wonderful, but I don't like Indian food or very hot weather. If I can't go to America, I think I'll stay in Britain. If the weather's nice, I'll go to Scotland or Ireland.
Paul: Yes, Scotland and Ireland are both interesting places, but if I can't go to India or Australia, I'll stay in England!

Exercise 5
My New Orleans Dream
I'm going to a special place with all of my friends
Down in Louisiana where the Mississippi ends
Gonna stay up all night and relax all day.
Down in my favourite city in the USA.

Chorus
I'm dreaming my New Orleans dream
Old time riverboats powered by steam
Jazz on the streets and houses from the past.
I'm dreaming my New Orleans dream
Sunny cafés with coffee and cream
Pack your bags fast – we're going there at last.
We're gonna spend the summer far away from school.
We're going on vacation. It'll be so cool.
We'll catch the plane tomorrow. I just can't wait to go
And once we're in New Orleans we won't want to come home.

(Chorus)

Where are the flowers? Where are the trees?
Where are the boats that travel down to the sea?
Where is the music and the warm summer breeze?
Come to New Orleans please.
We can catch a steamboat, we can sit in the sun
Down by the Mississippi we'll be having so much fun
There's singing and there's laughing, there's excitement everywhere
The streets are full of people and there's music in the air.

(Chorus)

20 Global Warming

Exercises 2 and 3
Presenter: Today I'm talking to Peter Whyles from the Climate Research Centre in London about global warming. Mr Whyles, how is global warming changing our climate?
Mr Whyles: Well, of course, temperatures are getting higher. We think the world will be three degrees warmer by the end of this century. The world is already warmer than it was 100 years ago and 1998 was the hottest year on record.
Presenter: What effect will this have on the environment?
Mr Whyles: Sea levels will rise because the polar ice caps are melting. This means that a lot of land will be flooded. By the year 2080, 25% of coastal towns around the world will be flooded. Unless we do something, we will lose lots of important towns and cities.
Presenter: What can we do to stop global warming?
Mr Whyles: We have to stop polluting the air. Pollution from factories, homes and cars releases most of the carbon dioxide into the air. Also, people are cutting down too many trees, especially in the rainforests. Trees absorb carbon dioxide. We need to plant more trees and stop people from cutting them down.
Presenter: Thank you, Mr Whyles.
Mr Whyles: Thank you.

21 What's Your School Like?

Exercise 2
Presenter: Kate
Kate: I like going to school very much. I've got lots of friends and most of the lessons are interesting. The best thing about my school is that there are some great school trips. Last year we went to France and this year we're going to Italy. The worst thing about school is definitely the homework. The teachers are nice, but they always give us too much homework.
Presenter: Simon
Simon: I like school, too. The thing I like best is going to drama lessons. I love acting and I'm in the school play every year. Maths lessons are the worst thing about school. I'm not very good at maths. I like my teachers, but I think that they are too strict.
Presenter: Adam
Adam: I don't like school at all. The only good thing about school is playing sport. I always enjoy sport, but I don't like any of my other lessons. Exams are the worst thing about school.

I hate them. My teachers are OK, but school is boring.
Presenter: Jennifer
Jennifer: I don't think that school is boring. I like going to school. The best thing about my school is the music club. I play the guitar and I'm good at singing, so I love the music club. The worst thing about school is the food. School food is horrible! But most of my lessons are interesting and the teachers are friendly.

22 Beverly Hills High School

Exercise 2
Sally Ann: Where is Beverly Hills High?
Tom: It's in California, USA. It's about 25 kilometres from Los Angeles.
Sally Ann: What are the students like?
Tom: Lots of kids at Beverly Hills High want to be famous and some of the students have famous parents. But many kids at Beverly Hills go there just because it's a good school. 96 per cent of Beverly Hills students go to college or university when they finish.
Sally Ann: What's special about Beverly Hills?
Tom: Everyone knows it's a good school for drama, but it's also good for sports. There are 45 school sports teams. There are also lots of clubs for music and dance.
Sally Ann: It must be a very popular school. Is it big?
Tom: It's an average size American high school. There are about 2000 students and 118 teachers.
Sally Ann: Do you have to be American to go to Beverly Hills High?
Tom: No, you don't! 34 per cent of the students are from other countries. Many of the students speak more than one language. You can hear 58 different languages at this school!

23 Coral Reefs

Exercise 2
Interviewer: Today I'm talking to Mary Kingsley from the Coral Conservation Society about the damaged coral reefs in America. Mrs Kingsley, how bad is the problem?
Mrs Kingsley: The problem is very bad. A lot of the reefs around America are extinct. In Jamaica, the coral reefs are disappearing very quickly. We must do something to stop this.
Interviewer: What can we do?
Mrs Kingsley: There are lots of things we can do. We must keep the reefs clean and stop putting rubbish into the sea. We must also stop fishing near the coral reefs. People like to visit coral reefs because they are very beautiful. Tourists mustn't leave rubbish or mustn't disturb the water around the reefs.
Interviewer: Can coral reefs grow again?
Mrs Kingsley: Yes. If we protect the reefs, they can grow back. At the moment, we are growing coral to plant in the damaged reefs.
Interviewer: Thank you, Mrs Kingsley.
Mrs Kingsley: Thank you.

24 An Interesting Country

Exercise 2
Presenter: So, what is Scotland famous for?
Simon: Scottish people are very proud of the poet, Robert Burns. He died over two hundred years ago, but every year, on his birthday, people celebrate Burns Night. And on New Year's Eve, they sing his most famous song, Auld Lang Syne.
Kate: Yes, that's right. The Scottish name for New Year's Eve is Hogmanay. At midnight, people play the bagpipes. The bagpipes are Scotland's national instrument and you always hear them on special occasions.
Simon: Scotland is famous for its food, too. The traditional meal is haggis, a special sausage made from meat and animal fat.
Kate: And Scotland's national costume is very strange. Men wear kilts. Kilts are made from special checked fabric called tartan. What else is Scotland famous for?
Simon: Well, Alexander Graham Bell was Scottish. He invented the telephone.
Kate: Oh yes, and the writer, Robert Louis Stevenson was Scottish, too. His stories, Jekyll and Hyde and Treasure Island are very famous.
Simon: And Scotland is the home of the Loch Ness Monster. Not everyone believes in the monster, but many people say that they sometimes see a strange animal swimming in the lake, Loch Ness.
Kate: Hmm, I'm not sure that I believe in the Loch Ness Monster, but I like Scottish dancing. The traditional Scottish dance is called the Highland Fling. It's a very lively dance. Would you like to try it, Simon?
Simon: Er, no thank you. I'm not very good at dancing.

Exercise 4
Rebecca: Here we are in Scotland. What shall we do for Burn's Night?
Steve: Well, we've got to have a haggis.
Rebecca: OK. Shall we make our own haggis or buy one?
Steve: We can make our own.
Rebecca: All right, what do we need?
Steve: We need some chopped meat.
Rebecca: OK, what sort of meat?
Steve: Lamb. We also need some liver, some heart and lots of animal fat.
Rebecca: Yuk! Let's not have a haggis.
Steve: What can we eat then?
Rebecca: Let's buy some turnips and potatoes. They're the right vegetables for Burn's Night. We can eat them with some chicken and beef.
Steve: That sounds a bit boring. Why don't we go out for a meal instead?
Rebecca: Good idea. And how about going to see the fireworks in the park afterwards?

25 A Typical English Person

Exercises 2 and 3
Helen: What do you think, Tom? Are you a typical English man?
Tom: I don't think so. For a start, I don't like tea. All English people should like tea, but I don't. I prefer coffee.
Helen: So do I. But what about food? Do you like fish and chips?
Tom: Oh yes. I love fish and chips. I know they are bad for you, but they taste great. I have fish and chips every week.
Helen: Really? I don't like them very much. I prefer curry.
Tom: Well, curry is more popular in England than fish and chips so perhaps you are more English than I am. What about football? Which is your favourite team?
Helen: I haven't got a favourite football team because I hate football. My favourite sport is tennis. I think it's much more interesting than football, don't you?
Tom: Of course I don't. Football is the most exciting sport in the world. Tennis is really boring.
Helen: Well, what about animals? England is supposed to be a nation of animal lovers. Do you like cats or dogs?

Tom: Cats. Dogs are OK, but you have to take them for walks. I think that cats are much better.
Helen: So do I. At least we agree on something. Do you like living in England?
Tom: Yes, but I hate the weather - it's awful! It's always raining and I hate rain. I don't like English weather at all.
Sally Ann: Neither do I. You're right - the weather is definitely the worst thing about living in England.

26 Fox-hunting

Exercises 2 and 3

Wendy: Fox-hunting is very cruel. Some people say that it's a sport, but it isn't. Lots of dogs chase after one fox, so the fox can't escape. Foxes are beautiful animals and it is wrong to kill them for fun. When people kill animals for meat, they die quickly and don't suffer much. In a fox-hunt, the fox dies slowly and it is very painful. Fox-hunting is cruel for dogs, too. Sometimes they get hurt badly.
Stephen: A lot of people say that fox-hunting is cruel but I don't agree. I live on a farm and foxes often kill our chickens. There are too many foxes in the countryside, so fox-hunting is important. Some people think it's kinder to kill foxes with poison, but this is dangerous because it spreads disease and pollutes the environment. It's natural for dogs to kill foxes and it's safer.

27 Your Favourite Sport

Exercise 2

Presenter: What's your favourite sport, Kate?
Kate: It's an American sport. Two teams play against each other. There are five players in a team. This game is fast and exciting. Most people who play this sport are very tall. For example, Shaquille O'Neal is two metres, twelve centimetres tall.
Presenter: Simon
Simon: My favourite sport is an American sport, too. There are 11 players in a team and the players have to wear shoulder pads and helmets. There are four quarters, which are 15 minutes long. The playing field is 110 metres long and 49 metres wide. At each end there is a goal post. Goal posts in this sport are three metres high.
Presenter: Jennifer
Jennifer: My favourite sport isn't American. People play it in more than 100 different countries. Usually, one person plays against another person, but sometimes people play in teams of two. You don't kick the ball in this game. You hit it with a racquet. The ball is very small. It's only seven centimetres wide.
Presenter: Adam
Adam: This is one of the most popular games in the world. There is a big championship every four years, when teams from different countries play against each other. People play this game on a pitch. The game has two halves, which last 45 minutes. It is a very old game. It comes from a Chinese game, which is 2,500 years old.

28 The Band

Exercise 2, Part 1

Teacher: This month, we're raising money for animal charities. I want you all to think of a way to raise money.
Presenter: Later
Jane: What are you doing?
Andy: We're forming a band. We're going to have a concert for the charity.
Natasha: That's a brilliant idea.
Andy: Dave is really good at playing the guitar, but I'm not very good at singing.
Natasha: I'd like to be a singer. Let me try.
Dave: What are you going to do for the charity, Jane?
Jane: I'm not sure yet.
Dave: Do you want to make some posters and tickets for our band?
Jane: Okay, and I can sell them for you.
Natasha: What do you want me to sing?
Andy: We're doing 'Angels' by Robbie Williams.
Natasha: And through it all ...
Jane: (thinks) Oh no, she's terrible.
Natasha: I really enjoyed that. What shall we try next?
Andy: (thinks) That sounded terrible. What are we going to tell her?
Presenter: Dilemma
What must Andy, Dave and Jane do?
a) Tell her that her singing is terrible and she must leave the band.
b) Let her stay in the band so that she doesn't get upset.
c) Persuade her to do something else for the charity.

Exercise 4, Part 2

Jane: Natasha, I know you want to sing, but I'm not very good at drawing. Can you help me with the posters instead?
Natasha: Well, okay. Sorry, guys I'd like to be in the band, but I have to help Jane.
Andy: That's okay.
Dave: Don't worry.
Presenter: Two weeks later.
Jane: The tickets are selling really well.
Natasha: Yes, we're making loads of money.
Boy: Two tickets please.
Natasha: That's five pounds please. Guess what? That's the singer in the band Gameboy.
Jane: They're a really good band.
Presenter: After the concert
Andy: We were great! We must do another concert.
Dave: Good idea!
Boy: Hey Dave. You're good at playing the guitar. Would you like to join our band?
Dave (thinks): Gameboy are the best band in the area. But what about Andy?

Exercise 5

I stayed in the band with Andy but Gameboy gave us free tickets to their concert. It was great!

29 The End of Term

Exercise 2, Part 1

Natasha: It's sports day in a few weeks. Do you think you'll get into the team?
Jane: I really like running. I hope I can get into the sprinting team.
Andy: Me, too.
Dave: I'm quite good at the high jump. I was in the team last year.
Presenter: Later
Jane: Here's the list of the teams for sports day. Great, I'm in the sprinting team.

Andy: I can't believe it. I'm not on the list.
Dave: Nor am I.
Natasha: Me neither.
Andy: Well done, Jane.
Jane: Thanks, but it's a shame that you aren't in the team with me.
Dave: I know. I'm so disappointed.
Natasha: Don't worry Dave. While Jane's training we can all relax and enjoy ourselves.
Presenter: Later
Andy: We're going to the cinema tonight. There's a really good film on. Do you want to come?
Jane: I'd love to, but I can't. I've got to stay at school for sports practice.
Jane (thinks): Natasha was right. They're enjoying themselves, but I have to do training. I don't want to be in the team.

Exercise 4, Part 2
Jane: I think I'll tell Mrs Williams that I don't want to be in the team. I'm fed up of training.
Andy: You really wanted to be in the team. You can't stop because we're not in it. We'll cheer for you.
Presenter: On sports day
Natasha: Good luck, Jane.
Jane: Thanks, I'm really nervous.
Dave: Don't be nervous. You're really good at sprinting.
Andy: Yes, you can do it.
Teacher: On your marks, get set, go!
Natasha: Come on, Jane.
Dave: She's winning.
Andy: She's done it!
Natasha: Well done, Jane!
Presenter: A week later
Natasha: Hooray. It's the last day of school.
Jane: I'm really excited about the holidays.
Dave: Yes, no school for six weeks.
Andy (thinks): I really like Jane but I won't see her for six weeks. I have to ask her out today.
Natasha: Let's celebrate by getting out the new Leonardo DiCaprio video. We'll have a girls' night. No boys allowed.
Jane: That's a brilliant idea. I'll bring some chocolate and popcorn.
Presenter: Later
Andy: Do you want to come to the cinema with me tonight - on a date?
Jane (thinks): I really like Andy, but I've promised Natasha I'll see her tonight.

Exercise 6, Part 3
Jane: Sorry Andy, I've promised Natasha I'll see her tonight.
Andy: Okay. Maybe we can go another day.
Presenter: Later
Natasha: Why are you sad? It's the last day of term!
Andy: I asked Jane out, but she can't come. I don't think she likes me.
Natasha: She really likes you. Why don't you and Dave come to my house tonight? I won't tell Jane. It will be a surprise.
Presenter: Later, at Natasha's house
Natasha: Can you answer the door? I'll get more lemonade.
Jane: Andy!
Andy: Surprise!
Dave: We heard there was a party here.
Presenter: Later
Dave: This film's really good.
Natasha: Yes, it's brilliant.
Andy: And the summer holiday will be even better.

Exercise 7
Summer's Coming
It won't be long till summer's here.
The most fantastic time of year.
No more books and no more school.
We'll be swimming in the pool.
It's gonna be hot even in the shade
So we'll eat ice cream and drink lemonade.

Chorus
Summer's coming, summer's coming.
Birds are singing, and the bees are humming.
The sun is out. The sky is clear
'Cos summer's nearly here.

We'll have a picnic by the lake
Chocolate, strawberries, crisps and cake
And when we've eaten all we can
We'll just relax and get a tan.
We'll go walking in the park
And watch a movie when it's dark.

We'll go down to the seaside,
Go to the funfair, get on a ride
We'll leave all our problems far behind
'Cos summer's here at last.
At weekends, we'll go to the coast
That's the place that we like the most.
We can play tennis on the sand,
Or walk together hand in hand.
And when the setting sun goes down,
We'll take a walk into the town.

(Chorus)

30 Oliver Twist
Exercise 3
Presenter: One cold night, nearly 200 years ago, a poor woman had a baby boy in a London workhouse. She died soon after he was born. The people in the workhouse called the baby Oliver. The dead woman had a locket around her neck with her picture inside it. The workhouse people didn't give the locket to Oliver. They decided to keep it because it was gold. Oliver didn't see his mother's picture. Life in the workhouse was difficult. Oliver never had enough food and he was always hungry. One day …
Oliver: Please sir, can I have some more?
Workhouse man: More? More! Greedy, horrible boy! No one ever asks for more food here. Your punishment is to clean the kitchen every day.
Presenter: Oliver decided to run away to London. He walked all day. When he arrived in London, he was very tired and hungry.
Artful Dodger: You poor boy! Would you like some food?
Oliver: Yes, but I haven't got any money.
Fagin: That's all right. We can buy it if you come and work for us. I'm Fagin and this is the Artful Dodger.
Presenter: Oliver was happy to have new friends. The next day, Fagin asked Oliver to go to work with the Artful Dodger.
Oliver: This is a strange place to work. Do you clean the streets?
Artful Dodger: Of course not. Now, we must be quiet so that I can take that man's wallet.
Oliver: (Thinking) Oh no! My new friend is a thief!
Mr Brownlow: Where's my wallet?
Man: This is the thief.

Mr Brownlow: I don't think that this poor boy is the thief. He looks very ill. I'm going to look after him.
Presenter: Oliver stayed at Mr Brownlow's house. A nurse looked after him.
Nurse: How are you today, Oliver?
Oliver: A bit better, thank you.
Nurse: (Thinking) Look at that picture on the wall. The lady looks like Oliver.
Presenter: A few weeks later
Mr Brownlow: Oh no! It's ten o'clock. I've got to take these books to the library and take this money to the bank, but I'm meeting my friend at half past ten. I don't have time.
Oliver: Would you like me to take them?
Mr Brownlow: Thank you very much, Oliver.
Presenter: In town
Artful Dodger: Where are you going, Oliver?
Oliver: I'm going to the library to return these books and then I'm going to the bank.
Fagin: No you're not! You're coming with us.
Presenter: Oliver had to go with Fagin and the Artful Dodger. That night, they visited a big house.
Fagin: The people who live here have a lot of money. The kitchen window is open. Oliver is small, so he can climb inside.
Oliver: I'm not going to steal from this house.
Fagin: Yes you are.
Presenter: Fagin and the Artful Dodger pushed Oliver through the window.
Woman: What's all the noise? It's a young boy!
Oliver: I'm sorry! Some thieves pushed me through the window. They wanted me to steal your money. But I'm not a thief. I live with Mr Brownlow.
Woman: Henry - look outside for the thieves. We can keep the boy here tonight and find Mr Brownlow tomorrow.
Presenter: The next day, Mr Brownlow arrived at the house.
Oliver: Mr Brownlow, I didn't steal your books and money. The thieves kidnapped me.
Mr Brownlow: I know. The police arrested Fagin this morning. I tried to find you yesterday. I visited an old woman at the workhouse and she showed me this locket. It belonged to your mother.
Oliver: You have a picture of this lady in your house!
Mr Brownlow: Yes! Her name was Agnes. We were friends a long time ago. Your father was very ill and I promised to help Agnes when the child was born. But when your father died, Agnes moved away and I didn't know how to find you. Now I can keep my promise.

Exercise 4
Oliver lived in a workhouse. He didn't have enough food so he asked for more.
He decided to leave the workhouse.
He walked to London.
He stayed with Fagin and the Artful Dodger.
The Artful Dodger tried to steal Mr Brownlow's wallet.
Mr Brownlow looked after Oliver.
Fagin and the Artful Dodger visited a big house and pushed Oliver through a window.
Mr Brownlow showed Oliver a gold locket.
Mr Brownlow promised to help Oliver's mother a long time ago. Now Mr Brownlow wanted to help Oliver.

Exercise 5
tried, visited, walked, promised, lived, pushed, asked, looked after, wanted, decided, showed, stayed.

31 A Christmas Carol
Exercises 2 and 3
Presenter: It was Christmas Eve.
Scrooge: Goodnight, Bob Cratchit. See you at six o'clock in the morning.
Bob Cratchit: But tomorrow is Christmas Day, Mr Scrooge.
Scrooge: Only idiots celebrate Christmas, but if you have to stay at home tomorrow, you can help me finish these letters tonight.
Bob Cratchit: Thank you, Mr Scrooge.
Presenter: At the Crachits' house
Bob Cratchit: Mr Scrooge was very kind. I don't have to go to work tomorrow.
Mrs Cratchit: Hmmph, Mr Scrooge is never kind. We don't have money to buy medicine for Tiny Tim because Scrooge is so mean.
Presenter: That night, Scrooge had a visitor.
Scrooge: Who are you?
Marley: I am the ghost of Jacob Marley. When I was alive, we worked together.
Scrooge: Why are you here?
Marley: I was mean too. Now I have to carry these chains. Three ghosts are going to visit you tonight. They have a lot to teach you.
Scrooge: Nonsense. I have nothing to learn from ghosts.
Presenter: Scrooge waited for the first ghost to arrive.
1st ghost: I am the ghost of Christmas past. Come with me. I have a lot to show you.
Presenter: The ghost showed Scrooge things from his past. There was a party. A beautiful girl was dancing. She was Scrooge's fiancée, but she married someone else because Scrooge was mean to her. Scrooge was very sad.

Next, the ghost of Christmas present visited Scrooge. He showed him Bob Cratchit's house. The family were having Christmas dinner. They didn't have very much food because they were poor, but they were very happy. Scrooge looked at Tiny Tim. He was very ill. Scrooge was worried about him.

The last ghost was the ghost of Christmas future. They returned to the Cratchits' house, but this time Tiny Tim wasn't there. The ghost showed Scrooge a graveyard. Scrooge looked at the grave of Tiny Tim. Bob Cratchit and his children were crying. Scrooge looked at another grave. No one visited this grave because it was the grave of a very unpopular man. The name on the grave was Ebenezer Scrooge.
Presenter: The last ghost disappeared and Scrooge was in his bed again.
Scrooge: What day is it?
Boy: It's Christmas day, of course!
Scrooge: Great – It's not too late! I must go to visit Bob Cratchit.
Scrooge: Hello, Bob Cratchit. I have a Christmas present for you and next year I'm going to pay you more money.
Mrs Scrooge: Come in and have Christmas dinner with us. There's going to be lots of food for everyone.
Presenter: Tiny Tim didn't die because Scrooge was very kind to him and the Cratchits always had money for food and medicine. Scrooge was never mean again.

32 Robin Hood
Exercises 2 and 3
Presenter: Robin Hood grew up in Sherwood Forest in Nottingham, England. His parents died when he was young and he had to kill deer for food. But the evil Sheriff of Nottingham owned the forest and he didn't like anyone eating his deer! One day …

Sheriff: Did you kill this deer?
Robin: I had to, sir. I was very hungry and there was no other food in the forest.
Sheriff: This is my forest and you killed my deer. If you steal from me, you must die.
Presenter: The Sheriff takes Robin to prison.
Presenter: Later, the Sheriff has a visitor.
Friar Tuck: I'm Friar Tuck. The King sent me to see the prisoner. I want to pray with him before he dies.
Sheriff: I don't like people visiting my prisoners, but I must do what the King says.
Friar Tuck: Thank you, sir. Let me cut those ropes and then we can leave.
Robin: Thank you, but why are you helping me?
Friar Tuck: I live in Sherwood Forest, like you. The Sheriff of Nottingham is not my friend. The forest does not belong to him - it belongs to everyone.
Presenter: Robin and Friar Tuck travel through the forest together. One day …
John Little: This is my bridge and no one crosses it without a fight.
Robin: That's OK. We love a good fight, don't we, Friar?
Presenter: Robin fights John Little and wins.
Robin: I won the fight, but you are bigger and stronger than me. Would you like to travel with us through the forest?
John Little: All right, but only if I can bring my friends.
Presenter: The men continue their journey. They meet an old knight. He is very sad.
Robin: What's the matter, my good man?
Knight: I was rich once, but now I am poor. I borrowed money from the Sheriff of Nottingham, but I cannot pay it back. He is going to take my castle from me tomorrow.
Robin: We can help. Meet us at the castle tomorrow, before the Sheriff arrives.
Presenter: Robin and his men take money from rich people travelling through the forest.
John Little: I'm sorry, sir. We need this money more than you do.
Robin: You are beautiful enough without this. We can take it for you.
Presenter: Robin meets the knight at the castle.
Robin: Here's the money. Now you can keep the castle. (Thinking) Who's that girl? She's beautiful.
Knight: Thank you. This is my daughter, Marian.
Marian: (Thinking) Wow! Robin is really handsome.
Presenter: Two weeks later, Robin and Marian get married.
Marian: Why are you sad, father?
Knight: I'm pleased you are married, but now I'm going to be alone.
Robin: You don't have to be alone. You can join my group of men.
Presenter: Next day
Friar Tuck: Robin, quick! The Sheriff of Nottingham arrested John Little for stealing from rich people. They are going to kill him this afternoon.
Robin: Everyone, come quickly. We must save John.
Presenter: Robin and his men arrive just in time.
John Little: Robin, you saved me!
Friar Tuck: If we can stay in the forest and eat deer, you can live.
Sheriff: All right, all right. I don't want to fight Robin Hood anymore. I never win!

33 The Hound of the Baskervilles

Exercises 2 and 3

Presenter: Many years ago there was a cruel man called Hugo Baskerville. He was in love with a girl who hated him. One night, he locked her in a room at Baskerville Hall. She jumped out of a window and ran away. Hugo rode after her with his hounds. He asked the devil to help him find the girl and the devil's hound ran after him. When people found Hugo the next day, he was dead. The devil's hound was biting his neck.
Sir Henry Baskerville is scared because of the story. He visits Sherlock Holmes.
Sir Henry: My Uncle, Sir Charles Baskerville died a few months ago at Baskerville Hall. The footprints of a hound were next to him. I must go to Baskerville Hall tomorrow.
Holmes: Don't worry. Watson can go with you.
Presenter: The men arrive at Baskerville Hall. Watson talks to some people.
Stapleton: Good morning. I'm Stapleton and this is my wife. We live the other side of the moor.
Watson: Hello. My name's Watson. I'm staying with Sir Henry. Do you know anything about the Hound of the Baskervilles?
Stapleton: Sometimes, when there are strange noises on the moor, people say it is the hound.
Watson: What do you think?
Stapleton: I don't believe the stories, but it's dangerous to walk across the moor at night. There are many swamps and you can die if you fall into them.
Presenter: Watson returns to Baskerville Hall, but Mrs Stapleton follows him.
Mrs Stapleton: Tell Sir Henry that he must leave. He is in danger here.
Watson: Why? What do you know?
Mrs Stapleton: I must go. Don't tell anyone I spoke to you.
Presenter: That night Watson sees a man watching the house. He goes outside to find him.
Watson: The man is hiding near here. Here are his clothes. I know that hat - it belongs to Sherlock Holmes.
Holmes: Hello Watson.
Watson: Holmes! What are you doing here?
Holmes: I'm watching Stapleton. I think that he killed Sir Charles.
Watson: Why?
Holmes: I can't tell you now. Stapleton is having a party tomorrow night and Sir Henry is going. We are going to wait outside Stapleton's house for Sir Henry to leave. I can't say any more.
Presenter: They see a hound running after Sir Henry when he leaves the party. Sherlock Holmes kills it.
Watson: Is this the Hound of the Baskervilles?
Holmes: No. This is Stapleton's hound. He knew about the story, so he bought this hound and hid it on the moor. When Sir Charles saw the hound, he died because he was so scared. Stapleton sent the hound out tonight to kill Sir Henry.
Presenter: They go into Stapleton's house to find him, but he isn't there. They find Mrs Stapleton locked in a room.
Mrs Stapleton: My husband locked me in this room because I wanted to tell Sir Henry about his plan. He saw you kill the hound and ran to the moor. You can catch him if you go quickly.
Presenter: Holmes and Watson see Stapleton on the moor.
Watson: What's happening?
Holmes: He fell into a swamp. He's sinking.
Presenter: They run to the swamp, but they are too late to save Stapleton.

Presenter: At Baskerville Hall
Watson: I don't understand. Why did Stapleton want to kill Sir Charles and Sir Henry?
Holmes: Look at this picture of Hugo Baskerville. He looks like Stapleton, doesn't he?
Watson: Yes, they have the same thin lips and cruel eyes.
Holmes: That's because they were related. Stapleton was really a Baskerville but he didn't tell anyone. Sir Henry is the last living Baskerville. Stapleton wanted to kill him to get Baskerville Hall.
Sir Henry: Well done, Holmes. You really are the best detective in the world.

Exercise 4
Presenter: Many years ago there was a cruel man called Hugo Baskerville. He was in love with a girl who hated him. One night, he locked her in a room at Baskerville Hall. She jumped out of a window and ran away. Hugo rode after her with his hounds. He asked the devil to help him find the girl and the devil's hound ran after him. When people found Hugo the next day, he was dead. The devil's hound was biting his neck.

Exercise 6
Rebecca: I love Sherlock Holmes. He's a brilliant detective.
Steve: Yes. The Hound of the Baskervilles is my favourite story.
Rebecca: Isn't Stapleton a horrible man?
Steve: Yes, he's horrible, but he's very clever. He wants to kill the Baskervilles so that he can have Baskerville Hall. He buys an enormous hound because he knows everyone believes the story of the hound of the Baskervilles.
Rebecca: Yes. No one thinks Stapleton is the murderer. They all think it is the evil hound.
Steve: But Sherlock Holmes knows the truth.
Rebecca: Yes, but he has to be very careful. He has to hide so that he can prove that Stapleton is the murderer.
Steve: And Stapleton runs away, but he forgets about the dangerous swamps and falls into one.
Rebecca: Yes, the murderer gets what he deserves!

34 Romeo and Juliet

Exercises 2 and 3
Romeo: Who is that girl over there?
Servant: I don't know.
Romeo: She's beautiful. I'm going to talk to her.
Romeo: Would you like to dance?
Juliet: I'd love to.
Lady Capulet: Juliet!
Juliet: I'm sorry. My mother wants to talk to me.
Romeo: Who is your mother?
Juliet: Lady Capulet.
Lady Capulet: You mustn't dance with that boy.
Juliet: Why not?
Lady Capulet: He is from the family that your father hates. He is Romeo Montague.
Presenter: Later, Romeo waits and listens outside Juliet's bedroom, because he wants to see her.
Juliet: I love Romeo, but he is a Montague and I am a Capulet. I don't want to be a Capulet if I can't be with Romeo.
Romeo: Marry me, then you can be a Montague.
Juliet: Romeo what are you doing here? Do you really want to marry me?
Romeo: Yes. I can speak to the friar tomorrow. We can get married in secret.
Presenter: A few days after the wedding

Lady Capulet: I have some wonderful news. Your father knows a young man who wants to marry you! His name is Paris. Your father is very pleased.
Juliet (thinks): They don't know I am already married to Romeo! I have to do something.
Presenter: Juliet visits the friar.
Juliet: I don't know what to do. It is better to die than to marry Paris.
Friar: This drink makes people sleep for a long time. I can tell your family you are dead and put you in the church. When you wake up, you can be with Romeo.
Presenter: The Friar writes a letter that explains everything to Romeo.
Friar: Please take this letter to Romeo. It is very important.
Presenter: The man tries to deliver the letter, but Romeo is not at home because he is meeting a friend in town.
Friend: Romeo, I have got some terrible news - Juliet is dead!
Romeo: I can't believe it. I must see her. I have to know if it is true.
Presenter: Romeo goes to the church to find Juliet.
Romeo: You are dead, but I still love you. I have some poison to drink.
Presenter: Juliet wakes up.
Juliet: Romeo, you are dead! There is no more poison in your bottle, but you have got a knife. I must die too.

35 Othello

Exercises 2 and 3
Presenter: Othello is a lucky man. He has an important job and a beautiful wife. Almost everyone likes him. But Othello has got one enemy - Iago. Iago is an evil man. He works for Othello. He wanted to be his lieutenant, but Othello chose Cassio. Now Iago hates Othello. Iago wants revenge against Othello and Cassio. One night, Iago goes for a walk and meets Cassio.
Iago: (Thinking) There's Cassio. He's a good soldier, but he likes alcohol too much. I've got a good idea.
Iago: Cassio, you work too hard! You must relax. How about a glass of wine?
Cassio: All right, but only one. I have to get up early tomorrow.
Presenter: Three hours later
Man: Ha, ha. Your nose is red. It looks like a strawberry.
Cassio: Idiot! No one jokes about me.
Othello: Who is making all this noise? Cassio – you're drunk! I can't have a lieutenant who gets drunk and has fights. You must leave your job.
Presenter: Next day
Cassio: Why was I so stupid? I loved my job.
Iago: Don't worry. Go and see Othello's wife and tell her you are sorry. Desdemona can ask Othello to make you his lieutenant again. He does anything for his wife.
Presenter: Cassio visits Desdemona. She agrees to help. But as he leaves the house …
Iago: Who is that man leaving your house?
Othello: He looks like Cassio.
Iago: That's strange! Why is Cassio visiting your wife in secret?
Desdemona: Othello, I was thinking about poor Cassio. He was a good lieutenant. Why not give him another chance?
Othello: Let me think about it. (Thinking) Why is she thinking about Cassio? Is she in love with him? Of course not! She loves me.
Emilia: Look, Desdemona dropped her favourite handkerchief. It's the one Othello gave her when they met - Desdemona!

Iago: Don't call her. They are busy. Give the handkerchief to me. I can return it later.
Iago: (Thinking) I'm going to put this in Cassio's room.
Presenter: Next day
Cassio: (Thinking) Where did this handkerchief come from?
Iago: What has Cassio got? Is that Desdemona's handkerchief?
Othello: (Thinking) Oh no, it's true! Desdemona loves Cassio. She looks sweet and honest, but she is a liar.
Presenter: That night.
Desdemona: Othello, is that you?
Othello: Yes, but perhaps you wanted someone else.
Desdemona: What do you mean?
Othello: I saw Cassio with the handkerchief that I gave you. I loved you, but you lied to me. Now you must die.
Presenter: Emilia comes into the room.
Emilia: I heard noises. What's wrong? Desdemona!
Othello: I loved her, but she loved Cassio. I killed her.
Emilia: Help! Help! Othello killed his wife.
Man: What happened?
Othello: She loved Cassio. She gave him her handkerchief. I saw him with it.
Emilia: No, she dropped the handkerchief. My husband took it.
Iago: Shut up, Emilia!
Emilia: I'm dying!
Man: Take Iago, men.
Othello: Yes, take him, but don't kill him. I want him to live and suffer. But Desdemona is dead so I must die, too.

36 Treasure Island

Exercise 3
Presenter: Jim Hawkins was a poor boy who lived with his mother in a guesthouse. One of the guests was very ill.
Jim: Mother, get the doctor. I think that this man is dying.
Presenter: Dr Livesey arrives.
Livesey: I'm sorry. It's too late. There's nothing I can do to help this man.
Man: The doctor's right. But before I die, there's something I want to give you, Jim.
Jim: It's a treasure map!
Presenter: The man dies and Jim shows his map to the doctor.
Jim: I'd like to find the treasure, but I'm too young and I don't know any sailors.
Livesey: I was a sailor a long time ago. I can come with you. But we must choose our other sailors carefully. We don't want any pirates on our ship.
Presenter: Jim and Dr Livesey go to see Captain Smollett.
Jim: We are going on an adventure to find treasure. We'd like you to be our captain.
Smollett: I can come, but don't talk loudly about the treasure. There are pirates in here.
Long John Silver: Did you say you were going on an adventure? You need a man like me. I'm the best cook in England. And I know other sailors who can come, too.
Presenter: The men begin their voyage.
Smollett: Jim, don't show your treasure map to anyone. I don't trust these men, especially Long John Silver. I think he's a pirate.
Jim: Really? I don't think that he's dangerous. He's only a cook.
Presenter: Later, Jim hears Long John Silver talking to another man.
Long John Silver: There's treasure on the island and the boy has got a map. When we arrive on the island and find the treasure, we can kill the doctor, the captain and the boy and steal the treasure.
Presenter: Jim finds Dr Livesey and Captain Smollett to tell them what he heard.
Jim: Long John Silver wants to kill us after we've found the treasure so that he can steal it.
Smollett: When we arrive on the island, we can tell the sailors that they don't have to work for the rest of the day. While they're relaxing, we can find somewhere to hide.
Presenter: The men arrive on the island.
Smollett: We can stay in this old house tonight - who are you?
Ben Gunn: I'm Ben Gunn. I've lived on this island for three years. Pirates stole my ship and left me here.
Livesey: There are pirates on our ship, too. We have to hide because they want to kill us.
Ben Gunn: I've got an idea. I have a boat on the beach. You can use it to sail to the other side of the island, where you can hide in the caves until the pirates have gone.
Jim: Let me find the boat.
Presenter: Jim finds the boat and returns to the house, but when he gets there …
Silver: Look men! It's young Jim Hawkins!
Jim: Where are the captain and the doctor?
Silver: We found them here and there was a big fight. But they couldn't win, so they ran away. Now you are our prisoner.
Presenter: The pirates take Jim's map. The next day, they go to find the treasure.
Silver: I don't understand. This is where the map shows the treasure. Why isn't it here?
Pirate 1: Long John Silver promised us treasure, but I don't think he's going to find it.
Pirate 2: Neither do I. And we worked hard to dig this hole. Let's make Long John sorry.
Livesey: Quick Jim, run!
Presenter: As the pirates fight, Jim and Dr Livesey run to the ship, where Captain Smollett and Ben Gunn are waiting.
Livesey: We're going home, Jim! I'm so happy!
Jim: So am I, but we haven't got the treasure.
Ben Gunn: Yes, we have! I found the treasure when I came to the island and I hid it in a cave. While you were with the pirates, we brought it to the ship. There's enough gold to make us all rich men.

Exercise 5

1	treasure	measure	either
2	know	how	so
3	fight	night	bite
4	young	long	sung
5	boat	note	coat
6	steal	meal	sail
7	really	early	nearly
8	choose	lose	loose